The Many Worlds of Herbert Hoover

Born: August 10, 1874
Died: October 20, 1964

Herbert Hoover rose through his own remarkable talents to preeminence as an engineer, humanitarian and public servant. A Quaker, orphaned at nine, with no formal schooling, he entered Stanford University at the age of seventeen. He gave up a lucrative career as engineer to become War Food Administrator to help the famine-starved civilians of World War I. From Secretary of Commerce he rose to President in 1929, only to see his country plunged into desperate crisis and the ideals that shaped his life lead him to overwhelming national repudiation. Here the author examines the many worlds of a man whose long life, though shadowed by tragic irony was rich in triumph and inspiration.

The Many Worlds of Herbert Hoover

by

JAMES P. TERZIAN

JULIAN MESSNER
NEW YORK

Published simultaneously in the United States and Canada by
Julian Messner, a division of Simon & Schuster, Inc.,
1 West 39 Street, New York, N.Y. 10018.

Printed in the United States of America

Library of Congress Catalog Card No. 66-10588

To the memory of
my father Paul

The Many Worlds of Herbert Hoover

ONE

HE STOOD ON THE RICKETY WOODEN PLATFORM long after the train pulled out of the station, a tallish, round-faced, husky young man with college written all over him.

In one hand he carried a battered satchel with a red and white varsity pennant stuck to it. In the other he clutched a narrow cardboard cylinder. His high-collared shirt, worn under a belted jacket, marked him a stranger to Nevada City, a small frontier town in the California foothills of the Sierra Nevada range.

The other passengers who had stepped off the train on that warm June evening in 1895 had already disappeared in the dust raised by buckboards and carriages. Only the college boy remained, a solitary, mildly distracted figure, like someone at an unfamiliar crossroad.

After a moment or two of hesitation he put his bag down, scratched his head, then plunged a hand into his pants pocket. The wad of bills—his entire fortune of forty dollars—was still there. It seemed to reassure him.

"Help ya, young feller?" An approaching stationmaster squirted a stream of tobacco juice that spattered just beyond the newcomer's bright yellow shoes.

"Yes, please. I want to get to a mine."

The stationmaster made no attempt to hide his skepticism. "You be a miner, then?"

"Yessir! A mining engineer!" The stranger held out the cardboard cylinder. "Just got my diploma . . . from Stanford University!"

The information apparently failed to impress. "Waal, mines shut down for the day, they be. Nuthin's open now 'cept saloons and hotels."

The young man licked dry lips. "Which one—I mean, which hotel is the cheapest?"

Another squirt of tobacco, another searching stare. "Try the Emerald down the street. And ask for a back room. Tonight's pay night and there's liable to be a ruckus hereabouts, there just might."

The room at the Emerald Hotel was small and not as clean as the visitor might have wished. But it cost only fifty cents a day and faced a rear alley, muffling somewhat the street shouts and gunshots now that darkness had fallen over Nevada City.

Before turning down the lamp, the young man sat up in bed, picked up the cardboard cylinder which lay next to his pillow and pulled out the rolled-up diploma. "Be it known to all presents"—he read the Old English script on it for perhaps the tenth time that day—"that Herbert Clark Hoover, having completed the required undergraduate courses as prescribed by the Sovereign State of California, is hereby granted the degree of Bachelor of Arts in Geology with all rights, privileges and honors—"

Herbert Hoover, then nearly twenty-one, looked up with a glint of satisfaction. Rights, privileges and honors! He had worked hard for that citation. But until it got him a job as a mining engineer, it would remain only a sheet of parchment, no matter how imposing the seal or impressive the wording.

But a job, any kind of job, was difficult to find in the summer of 1895. The business depression that had begun in the Eastern part of the United States two years before had, by then, spread to the economy of the West.

"Real nice, young feller," one mine manager drawled next day as he glanced down at the diploma. "But we're overstaffed in the front office as it is. No, not even a job in the pits. Try the Jeremiah."

It was the same story at the Jeremiah and the Four Clovers and the Happy Go Lucky, all "gold diggings" in the area. "We're firing, not hiring," they told him. Herbert also got the impression that the hard-bitten miners resented him, a dude fresh out of college. So he let his beard grow, dug out a pair of dusty jeans from his bag and laced on scuffed boots. The disguise helped until he spoke, at which time his subdued voice gave him away.

"Tell ye wot, lad," he was told one day by the superintendent of the Reward mine, "we're short-handed down below. Our mucker's had an accident, aye. Can ye handle a shovel and cart, then?"

Young Hoover never even blinked. A mucker, he knew, was at the bottom of the mining scale. But he couldn't afford to be choosey; not with only a couple of crumpled bills in his pocket. Rights, privileges and honors!

"When do I start?"

The hours in the pits were long, from eight in the morning until six at night. And the pay was short, two dollars a day and nothing if a man got sick or hurt. But he *was* working at his chosen profession, Herbert consoled himself, though not exactly at the level he had anticipated.

As a mucker, he shoveled a wet mixture of dirt and rocks into a rail cart, then pushed the load to an elevator at the foot of the mine shaft. For the first week he could hardly crawl back to his hotel at the end of the day to wolf down a meal and tumble into bed. But when his muscles toughened up and the calluses on his palms thickened he began to enjoy the job—rocks, dirt, water and all.

Below ground, the college-trained mucker was ignored by the other miners at first. Some even poked fun at his polite language, so free from their own Cornish expletives. But when they saw him push out five cartloads an hour where the man before had pushed four, they began to accept him as one of their own. Soon they were sharing their dinner pails with him and showing him how to make life more bearable in the damp pits below, including the technique of keeping warm by curling up inside a metal wheelbarrow heated by several miners' candles burning beneath it.

After a couple of months behind the carts, Herbert

was promoted to driller's helper with a raise in pay . . . four dollars a day. A step up, he agreed, but still a long way from the front office where a man could work with his mind in the full light of day instead of the lamp-lit night of the underground, and then only with his back and hands.

When Christmas time approached, Herbert Hoover, Stanford '95, took stock of his assets. He had one diploma, six months in the pits and a hundred dollars saved from his wages. The time had come to gamble it all. Not on the cards or dice or roulette, which, along with whiskey, made up many a miner's nightly entertainment. He decided to gamble his fortune on a trip to San Francisco. If ever he was to get out of the pits, the time was now. And the man to help him do it was Louis Janin, the best-known mining engineer in the West.

Herbert had met him a year ago while still in college. Janin had said then that he'd talk to anyone about a job in his organization provided two conditions were met. "First, the man must have actual field experience," the mining engineer had warned. "Second, there must be an opening in my firm."

Well, he had the field experience, Herbert assured himself as he checked out of the Emerald Hotel. As for the job opening, he just couldn't take the chance of being turned down through the mails. He'd go see Janin in person.

"One ticket to San Francisco, please." He pushed the money toward the stationmaster.

"Round trip, young feller?"

"Nope. One way."

Herbert Hoover wasn't planning to return to Nevada City, at least not right away and certainly not as a driller's helper. He was gambling now that his hard-earned diploma could make money not only for himself but for the firm which hired him.

TWO

HERBERT CLARK HOOVER WAS BORN ON AUGUST 10, 1874, in West Branch, Iowa, the second son of Jesse and Huldah Hoover. His birth was announced that particular morning by loud blows on the anvil of his father's blacksmith shop.

"Aye, and some day he'll make it all the way to the White House," Jesse called out to passers-by, "just like General Grant!" Normally a reserved man, the twenty-six-year-old blacksmith fairly popped the buttons off his muscular chest as the sweat poured down his beaming face.

Indulgent neighbors smiled. They knew as well as he that no man born west of the Mississippi had ever been elected President since the country was founded almost a hundred years before. Not likely that the precedent would be broken now, and by a poor blacksmith's son at that.

But the proud father was too excited to pay much attention to history. "Thee will find cider and doughnuts inside," he called out to friends and neighbors. "Oh, Huldah does well, by the grace of the Lord. Thou art kind for asking."

The "plain" language of *thee* and *thou* marked the young blacksmith as a member of the Society of Friends, or Quakers. For that reason also cider was the festive drink; in spite of heavy labors, Jesse Hoover drank nothing stronger than tea. And being a busy and thrifty man, he insisted on opening shop that day once the midwife assured him mother and son were out of danger. Horses had to be shod and plows repaired and wagon wheels rimmed with iron; in a farming community like West Branch, the absence of a blacksmith, even for one working day, could be a calamity.

Herbert Hoover—he was called Bertie as a child—took his first steps guided by his brother Theodore, or Tad, three years his senior. The brothers were joined by a sister, May, born two years later.

The tiny two-room cottage where the Hoover children were born proved no match for the growing family; shortly after May's birth, Jesse bought a four-room frame house not far from the shop. As Quakers, they lived simply, forsaking material show for spiritual gain; also due to economic necessity, for money was hard to come by in rural Cedar County. Like their neighbors, the Hoovers raised most of their food, wove much of their cloth and made their own soap. There was little luxury among the Friends of West Branch; or poverty, for that matter.

Bertie grew up under the influence of strict Quaker discipline. He and his brother and sister were taken to religious meetings even before they could walk. These were solemn devotions, held in near silence except when a Friend was moved by "inner light" to express kinship with the Divine Maker.

Mrs. Hoover, the former Huldah Minthorn, taught her children the Friends' gentle way of life, by both example and persuasion. Were they honest in all their dealings? Did they work willingly with others? Did they believe in freedom for the next person, regardless of his race or creed? Did they so conduct their lives as to make the world a better place in which to live?

To a small boy squirming restlessly on a hard wooden bench, these Quaker ideals probably meant very little at the time. Yet they became an integral part of Herbert Hoover's character, and shaped his adult decisions in a world far more complex than the one he knew as a child. They brought him many quiet satisfactions; also more than his share of problems.

In other respects, Bertie's early years were full of the joys and sorrows of growing up. He splashed in the "ol' swimming hole" in summer and slid down Cook's hill on homemade sleds in winter. He hunted rabbits with crackerbox traps and angled for catfish with butcher twine and penny hooks. Frogs and lizards, trophies of explorations along the riverbank, popped out of his pockets. He heard the chilling hoot of the owl at night and snuggled under warm quilts when blizzards swept over the Iowa plains. And in the fall of 1880, at the age of six, he took part in his first political rally—racing up and down Main Street during a torchlight parade, clamoring for the election of James Garfield along with the rest of West Branch, Republican almost to a man.

This happy existence was rudely shattered that winter when a typhoid epidemic swept through the county, leaving a score or more dead in its wake, among them the village blacksmith.

"Thee are without a father now," a sorrowing Huldah Hoover told her three children. "But with the Lord's help and our own will, we can manage." Herbert, barely five, could not fully comprehend her loss, May even less. Only ten-year-old Tad shared his mother's grief.

Jesse Hoover had left behind a pitifully meager "estate"—a small house, a blacksmith shop which was sold after his death and a thousand-dollar insurance policy. But Huldah, being a far-sighted woman, placed her reserve funds, such as they were, in trust with an old friend. "For the children's education," she told him. "Never let it be said that Jesse Hoover did not provide for his loved ones."

Soon after Bertie was invited to spend a year at an Indian reservation in Oklahoma where his mother's uncle served as government agent to the Osage nation. Here the youngster went to school with Indian children. He also learned Osage lore: the making of bows and arrows, lighting fires without matches and tracking wild game. The great outdoors became part of his life from then on.

When Bertie returned to West Branch, another influence reached him—the exciting world of books. Up until then Quaker discipline had limited his reading to the Bible, school texts and a handful of novels read to him by his elders for their moral tone and religious example, and containing vivid attacks against "demon rum." In those days, the Friends' tolerance did not, in West Branch at least, extend to their children's reading lists!

His initial brush with "worldly" forces involved a copy of *Robinson Crusoe,* surreptitiously slipped inside his brother's homespun shirt. "Me and cousin George are going to read it aloud in the attic," Tad whispered. "You can be the lookout, Bertie."

Later, while the breathless eight-year-old stood guard outside the attic door, the adventures of the self-tormented castaway were unfolded in whispers loud enough for him to hear. In like manner, almost second-hand as it were, Herbert shared in the *Leatherstocking Tales* and *Uncle Tom's Cabin.* From then on, books were never far out of reach.

Bertie also liked to walk along the nearby Burlington railroad tracks, his eyes searching for bright pieces of coral and agate mixed with the crushed rock spread along the rail bed. Afterward he laboriously polished these "gems" on a grindstone, then ran a wet tongue over them, the better to show their markings to admiring friends. Thus were cast the shadows of coming events. The geologist of later life began his career as a boy explorer among the ballast of the Burlington tracks.

But tragedy struck the family again early in 1883 when pneumonia took the life of Huldah Hoover. This time Herbert was nine, old enough to feel the irreparable loss. Many years later, he sadly philosophized that life in those days was not only hard, it was often also short.

But it did not lack love. Quaker relatives on both sides of the family gathered in solemn council after Huldah's funeral to decide on the future of the bewildered orphans. Tad went to live with a relative on his father's side. May was taken by Grandmother Minthorn, Mrs. Hoover's mother. Bertie, tight-lipped and struggling to hold back the tears, put a small hand into the callused palm of Uncle Allan Hoover, who owned a farm on the outskirts of West Branch.

"The Lord giveth and the Lord taketh away," Uncle Allan observed on the way home.

"Amen," his wife, Aunt Millie, echoed.

The finality of his mother's death hit Bertie. He cried softly in his aunt's lap as the shuttered carriage drove through a blinding snowstorm. At any other time the blizzard would have brought joy to his boy's heart.

Time and love have a way of healing all hurts. When spring burst upon Burlington County, it brought along the kite season, mumps, streams full of trout, a broken finger and a traveling circus. Bertie took them all in stride. By the end of summer he was his old self again, so full of the joy of living that the past hardly ever intruded, and then only at night when the cry of a hoot owl reminded him of other nights spent under another and more familiar roof.

Changes came with bewildering speed during the next

year and a half. Bertie grew faster than Aunt Millie could let the cuffs out of his patched overalls. He lost some of his baby fat, though still retaining his boyish chubbiness. He did well at the West Branch Free School, a one-room affair which housed all eight grades. And of course there were chores, always chores: milking, haying, chopping wood and bringing in the harvest. In those days farm living was based on the biblical adage that "whatsoever a man soweth, that also shall he reap." A farm boy who wanted to eat and have a place to sleep had better believe in that admonition from Galatians!

Another turning point came in Bertie's young life just after his tenth birthday. It was an invitation from Dr. Henry John Minthorn, his mother's brother, of Newburg, Oregon. "We have recently lost our only son," the letter to Uncle Allan explained. "Although God has blessed me with three fine daughters, our family fairly cries out for a growing boy. Can thee send Herbert to live with us? We can provide him with a Godly home and endless opportunities."

Uncle Allan and Aunt Millie considered the offer. They were very fond of their nephew, and he of them. But Uncle Henry was, after all, a physician and principal of Newburg Academy, a Quaker school. Surely Huldah's youngest son would have a better chance with him in Oregon than on a farm in West Branch. Did Bertie agree?

Bertie did, since they put it that way.

So with many parting tears and nearly as many bundles of food, the somber-faced youngster was packed off on an immigrant train bound for the Northwest, in those days a seven-day journey by slow freight.

Quaker kindness met him at the other end of the line; also school, religious discipline and the inevitable chores. Somewhat to his dismay, Herbert found Uncle Henry to be a taciturn man, not given to much show of affection. On the other hand, his new aunt fairly overwhelmed him with attention while his three younger girl cousins giggled endlessly at their gawky country cousin.

Bertie's main job in Newburg was to look after the doctor's team of horses and keep his medical office in order. By the end of his fourteenth year he had added three more inches to his height and now stood five-foot-six. And as he grew in size and strength he lost his diminutive nickname. To his friends at Newburg Academy he became simply Bert, a husky youngster with a round face, a shy smile and fine, sandy hair, straight as straw.

He also came to understand his uncle better, especially when he accompanied him on some of his house calls. In the solitude of the outdoors, and with only the clip-clop of the horses' hooves for company, Dr. Minthorn became less reticent. From him Bert heard an intriguing variation of Quaker philosophy. "Pacifists we are, that is true. But what I say is, turn thy cheek once. And if a man smites thee, smite him back!"

Bert graduated from Newburg Academy at fifteen, but before he had much time to think about the future, he found himself packing again. Uncle Henry, as restless as the new Northwest, gave up his medical practice and moved to Salem, some thirty miles to the south, where he opened up a Quaker land development office.

Salem was a bustling little metropolis in 1889, with paved streets, hotels, shops and thousands of people, more than Bert had seen all his life. As office boy in his uncle's firm, the Oregon Land Company, he ran many errands around the city. But on weekends, he took to the surrounding countryside, hiking, fishing and camping out.

Office routine fascinated the boy. Naturally curious, he peered over the bookkeeper's shoulder until the exasperated gentleman, out of self-defense, taught him the fundamentals of his profession. He learned typing the same way from the office typist.

He also discovered the treasures of the public library, thanks to Miss Jennie Grey, the kindly librarian. One day she stopped in at the land office, saw Bert engrossed in a book, then brought him several volumes to help him along. Among his favorite classics were *Ivanhoe, Moby Dick, A Tale of Two Cities* and all the adventure stories of Robert Louis Stevenson.

Another frequent visitor to the Oregon Land Company was a man named Hobson, a local Democrat, who dropped in from time to time to trade political blows with Uncle Henry, an avowed Republican. Their arguments over the gold standard and the protective tariff —Uncle Henry was for them, Hobson against—turned the air blue with smoke and un-Quakerlike language. Bert listened, a wide grin splitting his face. As for his own leanings, he sided with the Republicans all the way. Thus the political twig was bent.

But the man who really set Bert's future career was Robert Brown, an engineer from the East who came to the land office one day in search of a guide to survey mining sites in the nearby Cascade Mountains. "Best take my nephew," Uncle Henry advised. "He knows the countryside around here as well as any native and comes at half the price."

Bert jumped at the chance. He had spent many week-ends hiking and fishing in the Cascade foothills, some fifty miles east of Salem. He would have gone along with Mr. Brown for nothing, just to be with someone from "the other side of the Mississippi."

As they hiked over the range, the engineer stopped from time to time to collect soil and rock samples. Anticipating the boy's curiosity, Mr. Brown told him he was looking for silver ore in the area.

"You mean you can tell there's silver around here just by poking at a bit of rock?"

"Not just a bit, son. Many bits, taken at different sites, at different levels." He held up several samples. "Geographically, these specimens have a story to tell, just as though words had been printed on them." He pointed to the layers with their various markings. "Oh, yes, a geologist can tell with remarkable accuracy the history of any mountain range, including its approximate age, organic composition and economic value. And from what I've already seen around here, I'd say there isn't enough silver in these hills worth searching for."

That spot analysis gripped the boy's imagination. "What . . . what does it take to become a geologist, Mr. Brown?"

"Curiosity, for one thing. Intelligence, for another. Judging by your questions these past few days, you've got your share of both, and then some. You also need a college education."

Upon returning to Salem, Herbert Hoover solemnly informed his uncle that he wanted to become a mining engineer, just like Mr. Brown.

For the next few weeks he read dozens of college catalogues and finally decided on Leland Stanford Junior University, a tuition-free school near San Francisco, named after the late son of Senator and Mrs. Leland Stanford. A new college, it was scheduled to open for the first time that fall.

But getting in was something else. Lacking a high school diploma, Bert had to take a set of entrance examinations to qualify. He did poorly in all subjects but mathematics, in which he scored extremely high, a fact that probably saved his academic career.

"Don't give up, Bert," the professor in charge of examinations consoled him. "These math scores prove you're college material. How would you like another crack at them, later on?"

Bert looked up, puzzled.

"Here's my suggestion. If you can afford it, come to Stanford before school opens in the fall. There's a certain Miss Fletcher there who runs a boarding school for students who need extra tutoring. Three months under her whip should get you ready for the exams. But the question is, do you want to get into college badly enough to work for it? And I do mean *work*!"

If the countryside surrounding Leland Stanford Junior University in Palo Alto, California, ever held any charm and beauty, seventeen-year-old Herbert Hoover saw little of it in the summer of 1891. For those three months his nose was buried in books in Miss Fletcher's boarding school.

"Veni, vidi, vici," his tutor intoned.

"Gallia omnia in tres partes divisa est," Bert recited, none too sure of himself. Latin drills were followed by English grammar, European history, world geography and physics. At night, he studied about the stars instead of peering up at them in youthful wonder. By day he conjugated verbs while his hands itched to hold a baseball bat or a fishing pole.

His ability to concentrate paid off; Bert was admitted that fall to the first freshman class of Stanford University.

He had come to Stanford with six hundred dollars, his share of his father's legacy. Half that amount had already been spent on board and room and tutoring at Miss Fletcher's. The thing to do, he decided, was to find an immediate source of income. Soon after classes started, he established a college newspaper route, then opened up a laundry pickup service which he later subcontracted to students less busy than he.

Thanks to his typing ability, he also worked part time in the school's administration office. A few months later, he was hired by Dr. James Banner, head of the school's geology department, as the latter's laboratory assistant at thirty dollars a month, enough to keep him from depleting his meager capital.

The busy freshman lived in Encina Hall, a men's dormitory, where he shared a room with another first-year student. Bert took all the math and science courses he could, since these were naturals for him. He did less well in English, history and languages, though the only course he flunked in college was German. His average was a solid B, more than satisfactory considering his many extracurricular activities.

One of these was baseball. He tried out for the varsity team in his sophomore year. But when his anxious hands fumbled more grounders than they caught, he cheerfully accepted another assignment—manager of the team. "Bert fielded a thousand in this position," one teammate later recalled. "We were the best-outfitted, best-scheduled college nine in the Bay area, with the best gate receipts of any college our size, all due to Bert and his passion for detail."

This passion for detail led him into some embarrassing situations. One day, while supervising admissions for a baseball game—Stanford had no enclosed field in those days and sentries had been posted to collect a twenty-five-cent fee from spectators—a breathless student rushed over to him with news that a "bearded, bushy-browed old fellow just breezed by with no thought of forking over two bits!"

Bert gulped. The "bearded, bushy-browed old fellow" was none other than Benjamin Harrison, former President of the United States, who had come to Stanford that spring for a series of lectures on government. The former President was now heading for the stands directly behind home plate!

The student manager ran over and promptly blocked the distinguished visitor's path. "Sorry, sir," he said, "but no one admitted without a ticket!"

Harrison arched his imperious brows in amusement. "Not even former Presidents of the United States?"

"Not even the President of the University!" This came out with a rush. "Somebody has to pay for uniforms and baseballs!"

Harrison tugged at his beard. "In that case, young man, here's a dollar. And keep the change. I have a feeling it will be put to good use."

Another time, when Bert was manager of the varsity football squad, an unexpected crowd of more than twenty thousand showed up for a game, far many more than the number of tickets printed! What to do?

"We set up an alley of our college boys from the box office to the gates and sold tickets for cash . . ." he wrote in his autobiography many years later. "At that time few bills were in use in California. We dealt in silver and gold. The cash piled up . . . to the extent it spilled on the floors. We had to rent a wash-boiler and a dishpan from nearby householders for the price of a free ticket."

His troubles, though, were hardly over. In rushing about, the student manager had completely overlooked the matter of supplying game footballs for the sold-out contest! "We had to delay the game for a half-hour while we sent downtown for two pigskins," he admitted. Incidentally, game proceeds came to $30,018!

Bert's penchant for money-raising came a cropper soon after when he booked Ignace Jan Paderewski, the great Polish concert pianist, for a campus appearance at a guaranteed fee of two thousand dollars. The ambitious impresario knew little about advance publicity, or maybe the student body knew even less about Paderewski. At any rate, the hall was only half filled. A glum Hoover counted the house, then approached the pianist. "We are four hundred dollars short," he apologized. "I will give you my personal note for the rest. Only please don't let us down!"

He need not have worried. Paderewski, with a disdainful toss of his leonine head, strode out to the grand piano, sat down and banged out a Chopin prelude, perhaps somewhat louder than the composer had intended.

Bert also became involved in campus politics. Early in his junior year, he became aware that student affairs were slowly but surely coming under the control of fraternities and sororities. Although making up only a minority of the college population, they had managed to corner most of the elective student posts. This situation, with its implied appeals to snobbery, disturbed many of those who lived in dormitories and private "digs."

"What we need in campus politics is a reform ticket," one of Bert's friends spoke up during a bull session in Encina Hall. Hoover agreed, as did several other students, including Ray Lyman Wilbur, who later became president of Stanford University, and Will Irwin, who was to become a noted journalist and biographer.

"But what chance do we stand against the frats?" Wilbur asked. "They're organized, we're not."

"Then we'd better start," Bert quietly suggested. "We're a month away from elections."

That month was spent in a spate of campus politicking, marked more by vigor than finesse. Candidate Hoover—he ran for student financial manager—was part of a slate running on "integrity, independence and an end to student indifference." Probably the first "in" group of its times!

For their forceful insistence on reform, the non-frat ticket was dubbed the "barbarians" by the opposition. Bert and his friends gloried in the name. They invaded every dormitory and rooming house with their campaign message. They held street parades. They tacked up posters. They sent out speakers to eating clubs and cafeterias. In the end, they swept to victory.

Not all of Hoover's college education was confined to campus life. He worked during summer vacations, profiting both financially and academically. At the end of his freshman year, for example, Dr. Banner recommended him for a job as a surveyor for a geological study in Arkansas. The following two summers, he was a member of mining expeditions in Nevada and California, where he served as supply officer, outdoor guide, surveyor, field curator and even transportation officer in charge of pack mules!

Herbert Hoover's college days took a delightfully

romantic turn at the start of his senior year. Until then he had been so busy with school and work that he had little time for dating. Not that he was unaware of girls or they of him. He was, after all, a campus leader, a tall, presentable young man just a shade under six feet. But he had yet to meet the young lady who could compete with his other interests.

That all came to a head-spinning stop in the fall of 1894. One day, soon after school started, Bert walked into the geology lab, where he found Dr. Banner talking to an attractive, brown-haired, blue-eyed girl named Lou Henry. "She's come to Stanford to study geology," the professor explained. "Would you show her about the laboratory, Bert, and tell her something about our program?"

His assistant could only stare at the girl.

"Bert—!"

"Yessir!" Bert pulled off his apron and dropped it absentmindedly into a sink. "Will you please come with me, Miss . . . Miss . . . ?"

"Henry." She smiled, trying to hide her amusement. "Lou Henry."

From that day on the big senior made it a point to be at the lab whenever he suspected the attractive freshman might be on the premises.

One meeting led to another. Bert soon learned that he and Miss Lou, as he first called her, had much in common. She, too, was born in Iowa; she was, as a matter of fact, born the same year as he. Both were fond of the outdoors and shared a deep interest in geology. They also went to school functions together, to concerts and plays and football games. At the start of 1895 it was common knowledge on campus Lou Henry was Bert Hoover's girl.

No one was prouder of him on graduation day than she. There was the tacit understanding between them that someday, in the not too distant future, they would get married. "When you finish school, Lou, and I find the right job," was the way Bert put it.

He had also told her about his sister May and brother Tad, and his obligations to them. May, then only seventeen, had come to live with Tad upon the death of Grandmother Minthorn last spring. In order to support her, Tad had dropped out of school and taken a job as a teletype operator in nearby Berkeley. Bert had promised himself that someday his older brother would go back and finish college if he had anything to say about it.

For all these compelling reasons—impending marriage, a sense of obligation to his brother and sister, and certainly to his own career—Bert set his immediate sights on a job. Since he was now a mining engineer, the logical place to look for work was in a mining area. Lou agreed, even though it meant separation.

On the day after graduation Herbert Hoover bought a ticket to Nevada City, counted out his remaining fortune—forty dollars in cash—and boarded the train. In one hand he carried his battered old satchel with the red and white Stanford pennant stuck on it; in the other hand he clutched his precious diploma. Behind him lay his university days; ahead of him, his future.

THREE

SIX MONTHS IN THE MINES OF NEVADA CITY HAD broadened Bert's shoulders, toughened his muscles and firmed his resolve to get into the professional side of mining, which was, after all, the reason he had gone to college in the first place.

As Christmas 1895 approached, he wrote Lou Henry that he was coming to San Francisco to look for a job. Could she join him and Tad and May for the holidays?

The four young people spent a happy week together, then hurried back to their respective routines soon after the first of the year. Lou returned to school, Tad went to his job and Bert went looking for one.

He saw Louis Janin first. The mining expert received him cordially enough but offered little help. "About the only opening we have now," he told the unhappy young prospect, "is that of a typist. And of course, a college man like yourself—"

Gloom disappeared. "I'll take it!" Bert snapped. "Just so I can be around when a suitable opening *does* come along!"

Janin smiled. The boy had gumption and for him that was enough. "We'll give it a try, Mr. Hoover."

Much to Janin's surprise, Bert turned out to be a

good typist and an excellent copyist—duplicating mining contracts, survey reports and charts. The young engineer studied every document given him, thus acquiring intimate knowledge of behind-the-scenes operations.

Meantime, he lived in Berkeley with Tad and May. On Sundays he traveled fifty miles to Stanford for long visits with his fiancée.

After about a month in his new job, Herbert was called in to Janin's office. "Enjoying your chores, Bert?"

"Beats the pits anytime!"

"That so?" Janin frowned thoughtfully. "Frankly, I hate to lose a man of your obvious talents."

Bert's face went white. "Something wrong, sir?"

"I hope not." The frown disappeared. "Fact is, we need someone to help out in one of our mines in Colorado. Someone who's familiar with paper work as well as pit operations. From what I've seen of your work these past few weeks"—Janin pointed to a sheaf of papers on his desk—"I'd say we found the right man. The job pays $150 a month and expenses. Think you can handle it?"

Bert was ready that night. After a long-distance call to Lou, he took the next train out of San Francisco bound for Colorado. He had finally made it as a mining engineer!

For the next six months, Herbert Hoover served as assistant to whichever supervisor needed him most. One week he helped the chief engineer, the next the paymaster or the construction foreman, then it was back to the pits with the chief engineer. In all these assignments he kept his mouth shut, his eyes open and his ears cocked.

Hoover was next sent to a silver mine in New Mexico, another Janin enterprise. Here he served as assistant to the superintendent. He ordered supplies, checked work loads, hired pit workers and even helped maintain order among the rough and ready border men who, after pay days, frequently punctured the night with hoots and hollers and sometimes each other with knives and six-shooters. It was a rough tour of duty, but the strapping young Quaker's no-nonsense attitude soon earned the respect of the pit men.

Bert was recalled to San Francisco early in 1897. Janin now put him through the administrative paces: mining law, international contracts, personnel procedures, equipment purchase—every career challenge in the book. His warmest rooter during this period was Lou, then completing her junior year at Stanford.

Bert's big break, the one he was waiting for, came in October of that year. A cable from the British mining firm of Bewick, Moreing and Company asked Janin if he could recommend an engineer who understood American gold mining practices well enough to put them to work in Western Australia. Janin called in young Hoover. "I hate to lose you, Bert. But the job pays six hundred dollars a month and expenses, an offer I can't match. My advice is that you take it."

Bert said he'd have to think it over. That night, on the back porch of Lou's dormitory residence, he discussed the pros and cons with her. Western Australia, he had been told, was primitive country and brutally hot, no place for a woman. They would have to postpone their plans a while longer, until the right job came along. She agreed, though with a touch of melancholy.

Many years later, Hoover looked back on the Australian move with a profound sense of gratitude. The job enabled him to free Theodore (Tad) to go back to college. He graduated in engineering and after a successful career returned to Stanford as Dean of the Engineering School.

The twenty-three-year-old Hoover made the journey to Australia the long way around, from San Francisco to New York by train, then by steamship to London, where he met with his new employers. He then boarded another steamer, passed through the Suez Canal and sailed on to Western Australia by way of the Indian Ocean. A momentous voyage for a young man who, until then, had never even been on the other side of the Mississippi River!

His main job was to assist the resident manager in the development of gold mines in Western Australia. Herbert found the place unbelievably hot, with temperatures soaring over 100 degrees, even at night. Rainfall was sparse, water scarce and roads practically nonexistent.

One of his first assignments took him to a mining camp called Coolgardie, a sprawling frontier town of metal sheds, wooden huts and dusty streets. The mine, he found to his regret, was more picturesque in name than profitable in operation; the veins of gold were of such poor yield as to make further digging worthless. He so reported to London. But in nearby Kalgoorlie, the veins proved to be wonderfully deep and rich. However, the lack of water, so necessary for separating ore from dross, nearly stumped the American engineer.

Nearly but not quite. Using ingenuity and patience, Hoover introduced a filter press system which recovered all available water, to be used over and over again, the first time such a device had been employed in gold mining.

Transportation was another problem. Automobiles, of course, had not yet been perfected; horses were few and expensive to keep in the bush country. His first journey into the interior was astride a camel whose "motion imparts aches to muscles hitherto unknown," as he wrote home, and whose "long neck enables him to bite one's leg unless he is constantly watched."

On one of these trips, Hoover examined an out-of-the-way mining prospect called the Sons of Gwalia, owned by Welsh interests. Suspecting that it contained a bonanza, he cabled London, urging Bewick and Moreing to buy a two-thirds share in the undeveloped mine at a cost of half a million dollars. His evidence so convinced his superiors that they went along with his recommendations and even appointed him manager at the princely sum of ten thousand dollars a year. Furthermore, they cut him in on a share of the profits. This practice, in subsequent years, amassed a considerable personal fortune for the American engineer. The Sons of Gwalia exceeded Hoover's fondest hopes. Over the next half century, it produced more than $55 million in gold and $10 million more in dividends.

Hoover's year-long performance in Australia brought still another dividend. Bewick and Moreing wanted to know if he would next accept an engineering post in China. But they warned him that the demands of the job were formidable. He would have to develop new mines in the Chinese interior and supervise the construction of an ice-free port at Chinwangtoa, a city on the Gulf of Chihli, now called Po Hai, in northeast China. He was also told that he would have to work closely with officials of the Chinese government, then caught in a power struggle between the old traditionalists and the new reformers. However, his salary was equally formidable: twenty thousand dollars a year and expenses. The "right job" had finally come along.

Bert sent two cables that day. The first went to the British firm accepting the assignment. The second he dispatched to Lou Henry asking if she would consider becoming Mrs. Herbert Hoover.

Her answer came back in record time, an ecstatic yes!

He hurried home, arriving in Monterey, California, Lou's home town, on February 9, 1899.

They made a handsome couple, the groom husky and tanned, the bride tall, slender and radiant. Though not a Quaker herself, she insisted on adopting her husband's religion.

The sailing schedule to the Orient made for some odd nuptial arrangements. Since the next ship for China was due to sail February 11, the ceremony had to take place on the tenth. Nor could they be married in the Quaker tradition; a full Friends' meeting was required for such an event and none would take place until the end of the month, long after the China sailing. Furthermore, not a single Protestant minister could be found in Monterey that day, so the marriage was performed by a Catholic priest, a friend of the bride's family, who received special dispensation to unite the Quaker couple.

They sailed off on their month-long ocean honeymoon completely innocent of the trials and tribulations they would find in the ancient land of mandarins and emperors.

The Hoovers' first view of the Orient dazzled them. Junks and sampans crowded around their ship as it steamed into Tientsin harbor. They could not tell where water ended and land began, for the bobbing harbor craft, nestling side by side, formed a single mass that seemed to blend right into the docks and warehouses on shore. Every boat teemed with life: children, dogs, peddlers and gulls.

The newlyweds traveled on to Peking, China's capital city some eighty miles to the northwest, where Hoover met his English colleagues and officials of the Chinese government. Contrasts in Peking bewildered the newcomers. The city glowed with temples and walls and the glittering winter palace of Tzu Hsi, the Dowager Empress. It also reeked with filth and disease, inevitable companions to poverty.

"You will soon learn to overlook the sores of China," the Hoovers were told by their Western friends. They never did. Rather, the young Americans developed a deep compassion for the nation and her people. Mrs. Hoover resolved to learn the language of the north country. In time she became completely at home in the Mandarin dialect, though her husband admitted he himself could learn no more than a hundred words.

The Hoovers eventually settled in Tientsin, on the Gulf of Chihli, where they rented a house in the foreign settlement, which was ringed by walls. They were soon to learn the practical reasons for these age-old defenses.

They also learned that China was divided into three classes: the Manchu aristocracy, which ruled the vast country; the well-to-do landowners and merchants, who comprised about five percent of the population, and the squalor-ridden poor, the peasants and city dwellers, who lived under the triple burdens of heavy taxes, eternal poverty and disease. This last group made up the overwhelming majority of the Chinese population, some 500 million in 1899.

Hoover knew that there had been reform movements from time to time, the most recent being the reign of Kwang Hsu, the young emperor who had sought to industrialize the nation. Hoover's present assignment, as a matter of fact, had been part of Kwang Hsu's program.

But the traditional Manchus, reactionary and bound to China's past, had effectively blocked progress. Shortly before Hoover's arrival in Peking, the reform emperor had been deposed by the wily Dowager Empress, figurehead of the ancient regime.

Even so, Bewick, Moreing and Company had decided

to go ahead with their project. There had been indications that the Manchu Dynasty would follow through on the modernization program so desperately needed by a country which, although on the threshold of the twentieth century, had its roots planted firmly in the fifteenth.

For a while it seemed as though all might yet go well. Yes, agreed Chang Yen-mao, the government's official in charge of the project, China was indeed anxious to build a modern ice-free port. No, the honorable "American mandarin" would encounter no difficulty in getting government help. Yes, it was most important to discover new mines, especially those producing gold.

Gold? Impossible! Hoover had taken pains to study China's economy. He told Chang the nation's primary need was iron, steel, coal, lead, zinc, copper and other industrial metals. But he argued to no avail. It was obvious that the reform regime had badly crumbled.

Nevertheless, between wild-goose chases in the interior in search of gold (which Hoover never found in worthwhile quantity, though he discovered coal deposits near Peking which rank among the richest in the world), he brought in Western experts and set about improving the port before winter locked them in.

Weather proved to be the least of his problems. The young engineer soon found his projects mired in graft, inefficiency and intrigue. The practice of paying "squeeze," the Chinese word for extra fees on top of labor and service charges, outraged his sense of sound business practices. As he later explained, he would have much preferred to pay salaries and wages and establish a profit-risk system more in keeping with his own concepts of free enterprise. But "squeeze" it was, and "squeeze" he paid in order to get the job done.

Hoover's problems were further compounded by hordes of European fortune hunters anxious to obtain mining concessions for their governments regardless of ethics. Therefore, to protect China and his own company against claim jumpers, the American drafted a mining law which he submitted to Peking. It granted foreign nations equal development rights, and the Chinese government a guaranteed share of the profits. Although little came of the decree, it was one of the first attempts to safeguard China against foreign exploitation.

This abuse had been going on for some fifty years prior to 1900. Russia had already carved out an economic empire in Manchuria and parts of Turkestan. Japan's Rising Sun shone on strategic islands off the China coast; it was later to extend its rays far into the interior. France, too, had found a sphere of influence in the Orient. The tea, rubber and rice plantations of southern China flourished under French rule and French profits, while the British lion haughtily stalked the jungles of Burma, which for thousands of years had belonged to the Chinese. To a lesser extent, Belgian, German and American interests had also taken root there. In the existing morality of the times, to invest in China meant establishing territorial claims and sending in troops and gunboats.

No wonder that many foreigners at the time were

looked upon with suspicion and distrust by those loyal to Chinese tradition. Even Christian missionaries, with their schools and hospitals, often fell under this hostile cloud.

Antagonism against Western influence reached a fever pitch in 1900, the year after the Hoovers landed in China. It was organized and directed by a secret society called I Ho Tuan, the mailed fist, or "The Boxers," as the foreigners called it.

Hoover himself said this about the Boxers: "Their avowed purpose was to expel all foreigners from China, to root out every foreign thing, houses, railways, telegraphs, mines, and they included all Christian Chinese and all Chinese who had been associated with foreign things. They believed they had supernatural protection from foreign bullets . . ." Fanaticism, wedded to cause, often bears violence as progeny.

And the violence that came to them, and to thousands of other Americans, Europeans and Chinese Christians, was the short but bloody uprising known as the Boxer Rebellion.

The Americans' first suspicions of trouble were aroused when the Chinese Imperial Army, stationed just outside Tientsin, presumably to protect the city, began to take a hostile attitude toward Westerners. Sensing an imminent crisis, Hoover called in his field engineers from the provinces. And just in time, because the Boxers began to move early in June, goading the Chinese armies ahead of them. They meant to capture Peking and, since Tientsin lay in its path, it, too, must be leveled. Besides, there were three hundred foreign civilians and fifteen hundred of their troops, hated symbols of the outside world, in that port city. The first shells exploded over Tientsin on the morning of June 10, 1900.

The men of the foreign sector called an immediate council of war. The defense of the area, about a mile long and a quarter of a mile wide, was put under the command of Colonel Wogack, an astute Russian officer. The colonel promptly gave Hoover the job of fortifying the settlement and looking after its food supply.

Hoover the engineer and Hoover the Quaker now confronted each other. He could not be a pacifist for long, not when enemy shells were bursting all around defenseless men, women and children. What was it Uncle Henry had said? *Turn thy cheek once. If a man smites thee, smite him back.*

Hoover quickly surveyed the situation. The first line of defense was already being breached by Boxer forces. He immediately ordered the construction of an inner wall built by sacks of wheat, flour, sugar—any material that could be dragged out of the huge warehouses near the harbor. Colonel Wogack stationed his troops behind these barricades.

Meantime, hundreds of Christian Chinese clamored for admission into the fortified area. Being "tainted" by the West, they too were marked for extinction. They were let in and put to work for the common defense.

Fortunately, food was no problem. A herd of cattle, quickly commandeered at the first shot, provided meat and milk for the beseiged inhabitants. But water was something else again. An important waterworks lay just outside the defense perimeter. Water patrols, led by Hoover himself, crept out at night to replenish the defenders' scant supplies.

Lou Hoover was also busy, scurrying about on her bicycle, giving comfort and aid to the frightened Chinese women and children. The settlement club was turned into a hospital where two doctors and a nurse worked around the clock to care for the sick and wounded.

The siege began in earnest the following morning, with twenty-five thousand Chinese troops and Boxers putting on the pressure. Shells pounded into the settlement. The order of the day was "Stick close to the barricades!" Even so hundreds within the compound were killed, many more wounded. In all, Hoover estimated that sixty thousand enemy shells and thousands of machine-gun rounds were fired at the defenders during that nightmare month.

As engineer in charge of fortifications, Hoover was never far from the defense perimeter, even as the Boxer fanatics closed in, street by embattled street. He slept when and where he could, between attacks.

"We must hold out, house by house if we have to," he exhorted, "until help gets to us from the outside!" Then he dashed off as a frantic messenger came up with news that the attackers had overrun a warehouse in the northern sector.

Lou Hoover, meanwhile, shuttled between the hospital and her home. Once, her husband remembered, "when a shell banged through a back window and blew out the front door, Mrs. Hoover . . . sitting in a side room playing solitaire . . . never stopped the game." She had been working all day at the hospital and was, apparently, too exhausted to move!

Another time, a Boxer shell exploded just across the street from their dwelling. This time, Hoover and John Agnew, his chief of engineers, dashed out and saw that the house of a Chinese friend, Tong Shao-yi, had been leveled. Screams of frightened children reached their ears. Unmindful of danger, the two men dashed into the ruins. They found Tong's wife and baby dead, the other children wailing in fright, and Tong himself in a state of shock. They carried them to the safety of Hoover's own home, where Lou took care of the survivors.

The siege continued week after week. When at last it seemed that the defenders had reached the limit of their endurance, the enemy shells suddenly stopped crashing overhead. After so intense a conflict, the strange silence brought a new wave of anxiety. Were the Boxers, finally, preparing an all-out assault?

They had their answer within minutes. A breathless messenger, waving an American flag, stumbled through the barricades with news that a relief column of United States Marines had driven off the rebels and were on their way to free the embattled captives!

Hoover described the timely rescue in his memoirs: "We climbed on the roof of the highest warehouse . . . and saw them coming over the plain . . . American Marines and Welsh Fusiliers. I do not remember a more satisfying musical performance than the bugles of the American Marines entering the settlement playing 'There'll Be a Hot Time in the Old Town Tonight.' "

The "hot time" of the siege continued for several more days, but at last a main column of rescuers arrived and drove the Boxers and Chinese troops into the hills, where they eventually sued for peace. Among those who took flight, incidentally, was Chang Yen-mao, the doublecrossing Chinese official who had smilingly assured Hoover that the Dowager Empress's government would cooperate in every way to modernize the port facilities of the Chihli Gulf!

With the demise of the government, Hoover found himself without a job, a situation which, at the moment, brought him a profound sense of relief. He and Lou returned to the United States in August 1900. Even so, his respite was brief, for Bewick and Moreing asked him to return to China and salvage what he could of company equipment from the ruins of the rebellion.

Hoover returned to the Orient early in 1901. However, Lou remained in the comparative safety of Japan while the young engineer, not yet twenty-seven, showed himself in a new light—the determined legal champion of bondholders who had invested in the China enterprise.

FOUR

"CHAOTIC" WAS THE WORD MOST OFTEN USED BY Herbert Hoover to describe his return to Tientsin. The Boxer Rebellion and its aftermath had made a shambles of the countryside.

Mining machinery leased to the Chinese government had been carted off as spoils of war by the Russian, German and Japanese troops, the very armies sent in to drive off the Boxers. American forces had appropriated harbor facilities and barges. Meanwhile, Chinese peasants had helped themselves to whatever the "liberators" had overlooked, even to ripping up railroad ties and tracks. Hoover's orders from his firm were clear: "Recover what you can, demand reparations for what you can't!"

His was certainly not an armchair job. That winter he sailed on ships that crashed through Chinese ports choked with ice; he rode for days on unheated troop trains; he even hiked over frozen plains when not a horse or a carriage could be commandeered. He tracked down foreign ministers in Peking, argued with technical experts in Tientsin and stood firm in the face of threats from military commanders all over North China. In the end, the engineer-turned-diplomat succeeded in putting together the vast commercial jigsaw puzzle and even convinced the Chinese peasants to return stolen rail sections by offering to buy them back at five dollars each!

The young American's ability to set his company's house in order so impressed Bewick and Moreing that they offered him a junior partnership in the firm at a substantial boost in salary plus a share of the company profits.

Bert and Lou Hoover weighed the proposal carefully. They had set their hearts on returning to California, where they hoped to settle down and raise a family. But the London offer promised financial security, travel and, most important, an opportunity for career growth.

"Take it," Lou urged. "We'll make our home wherever your job takes you."

It turned out to be a seven-year assignment that delighted the Hoovers' penchant for new places and experiences. First, however, they returned to America for a family reunion with Tad and May. They also made plans to build a cottage in the San Francisco Bay area in order to establish their American residency. Then they continued on to London, where Hoover quickly became a part of the firm's corporate structure. It very nearly proved his financial undoing.

One morning, after about two months on the job, Hoover found a letter on his desk marked "private and confidential." He opened it, then sat back in stunned silence. One of the firm's junior partners, A. S. Rowe, had just confessed to embezzling more than a million dollars' worth of stockholder funds by forging worthless stock certificates! Moreover, he had topped off his confession with a threat of suicide!

Hoover was, at the time, the ranking company representative in London since Moreing was in Manchuria and Bewick had taken off to the Canadian wilds on a hunting trip. He knew neither senior partner could be reached for days. Meantime, a life was at stake, to say nothing of the company's reputation.

His first move, in that emergency, was to alert the police in order to head off Rowe's threat of suicide. Then he called in the firm's lawyer and a few trusted business associates and told them about the confession. They were as shocked as he—also wise to the ways of British law. "The firm has no legal liability for financial losses since they were due to forgeries," he was told.

"Liable or not," Hoover countered, "we have an obligation to make good every dime of the stockholders' losses."

The lawyer smiled. "*Tuppence,* Mr. Hoover, would be more appropriate to British currency."

That wry comment broke the tension. The emergency council agreed to quietly inform the company's stockholders of Rowe's forgeries and assure them that their investments would be protected. Cables to that effect were then sent off to the absent senior partners.

Hoover's quick action turned the tide. Rowe was apprehended before he could carry out his suicide threat. Panic was averted among investors. As soon as word reached Mr. Bewick and Mr. Moreing, they cabled back their entire willingness to go along with Hoover's plans. For his part, the young junior partner insisted on paying his pro-rated share of losses, though it drained his savings at the time and cut into his income for several years thereafter.

A change of scenery quickly put this unpleasantness behind. Anxious for new assignments, Hoover asked to get out into the field once more. The young couple—neither had yet reached thirty—circled the globe five times in the next seven years and visited more than twenty countries.

These long voyages gave him a fine opportunity to read. His baggage never lacked for books: Shakespeare and Schiller, Goethe and Confucius, Poe and Plato, Hugo, Dumas and Zola, the great social and political writers of the French Revolution—all were grist for his inquiring mind.

He also wrote a number of engineering articles during these years. He based them largely on his duties, which included the evaluation of mining prospects, modernizing old diggings, hiring qualified experts and supervising the construction of roads, rail lines and mining camps. In a casual footnote to that period, he confessed that he "made several contributions to professional journals and societies on technical phases of our work. They are dull reading for laymen."

For laymen, perhaps, but in the engineering world they increased his stature. His ability to bring new life to discarded mines soon earned him a reputation as the "doctor to sick companies," and wise investors knew his shrewd opinions on a project often meant the difference between profit and loss. While still in his mid-thirties Herbert Hoover was widely recognized in his profession as an outstanding mining engineer and administrator. But as far as the general public was then concerned, the name Herbert Hoover meant little or nothing.

It was during this period also that the Hoovers turned their attention to a long delayed goal—raising a family. Their first son, Herbert, Jr., was born in London on August 4, 1903. However, the event interfered with neither the young father's career nor the mother's determination to accompany him on his global assignments. Just five weeks after the baby was born, Lou Hoover bundled her infant into a hand basket and carried him aboard a steamer bound for Australia.

That family vignette, complete to the same hand-carried basket, was repeated four years later with the birth of their second son, Allan, also in London. With Herbert, Jr., now toddling between them, the proud parents boarded another steamer, this one bound for Burma. It was to be one of Hoover's most profitable—and challenging—assignments for Bewick and Moreing.

Burma is a tropical country nearly the size of Texas, lying between India to the west and China to the north. On the map it looks somewhat like a diamond-shaped kite, even to a tail of land which trails down the western coast of the Malay Peninsula. Today, Burma is a republic. In 1907 it was part of British India, a land noted for its fabled cities of Rangoon, Moulmein and Mandalay, for its mighty Irrawaddy River, for the setting it provided for many of Rudyard Kipling's tales, and for its contrasts of wealth and poverty, by-products of both colonialism and feudalism.

Hoover had come to Burma at the invitation of a British-educated native prince who ruled the small province of Shan. "I want you to look into an abandoned mining area just fifty miles from the China border," he told the American on his arrival. "The Ming Dynasty once mined great lodes of silver there. But today it lies idle. I am told you can perform miracles with mines that no longer produce."

"Not miracles," Hoover corrected. "I try to make them profitable only if I am convinced there is something of value in the mines."

"You must be convinced," the prince pleaded. "My people are desperately in need of work, my province greatly in need of industry." He might have added that his coffers were nearly empty, his palace somewhat seedy and his wives—he had twenty—even more so. No way for royalty to live, he seemed to imply.

Next day, Hoover and another engineer named Clark set out on horseback through the rain-drenched teak forests of Shan while monkeys and parrots chattered in alarm at the sight of two strange men and beasts poking their way through their jungle domain. The engineers finally came to a large clearing dotted with huge heaps of slag, evidence of past excavations. A cursory examination proved that the slag still retained a fair amount of lead, the base metal from which silver is refined. It was Hoover's guess that it might be profitable if only some way could be found to bring in heavy equipment.

Further investigation unearthed several overgrown pit openings, which Hoover and Clark entered gingerly. Their candles threw weird shadows about them while the dust of centuries sprinkled down over their helmeted heads. Hoover judged the shafts to be hundreds of years old, no doubt dating back to the Ming Dynasty, which was at its height about the time Columbus discovered America.

The two men descended deeper into the pits until they were wading through knee-deep pools of water. They plunged on, drawn by unmistakable signs of rich veins of lead, especially below water levels. "Probably why the pits were abandoned in the first place," Hoover surmised. "No way could be found to drain these pools." He tried to shake himself dry. "I tell you, Clark, these mines can be worked. The trick is to first pump the water out, shore up the tunnels, dig the ore, then find a way to get it through the jungles and to a seaport."

"Some trick," his companion snorted in the damp darkness. "Rangoon is what, five hundred miles to the south?"

Hoover nodded thoughtfully. He was already transforming this isolated area into an industrial complex.

On his return he gave his report to the Prince of Shan. To get the mines working again, he told him, it would take twenty thousand men two years to build a railroad through the jungles from Mandalay to the mine site, and about two million dollars before a ton of ore could be floated down the Irrawaddy River to Rangoon.

"I can raise the work force, Mr. Hoover," the Prince said, his eyes gleaming at the prospect, "if you can raise the capital."

Hoover said he would try. Next month he was on his way to London for consultations with Bewick and Moreing. This time he dropped off Mrs. Hoover and the two boys in California to give them a taste of life in America.

Hoover had so much faith in the Burma venture that he himself invested heavily in it. He was certain he had come across one of the great lead and zinc deposits of the Far East.

In time, the Burma mines turned out to be immensely successful. Lead and zinc poured out to a metal-hungry world. Over the next thirty years they produced 1,500,000 tons of lead, 135,000,000 ounces of silver and great quantities of zinc, all with a total value of $350 million!

The Prince of Shan and his province, of course, prospered. So did the investors who had risked their money in the enterprise.

Hoover noted that the wages paid to local natives at the time (1908) were above any standard the jungle had ever known, and the first money thousands of them had ever had. He did not say what the actual wages were, but some years before, when he was in China, he wrote that the going rate for common mine labor then was six cents a day. Admittedly, wages did not have to be very high in those days to be above jungle standards.

Some of Hoover's later critics leveled the charge that he had built his fortune on the backs of cheap labor. But one of his biographers, fellow Quaker David Hinshaw, gave a partial answer to this charge. He wrote that Hoover was motivated primarily by the Quaker philosophy which sought to create a social and economic system which would so function as to sustain and enrich life for all.

Hoover himself emphasized this point when, looking back on the Burma project, he wrote, "We built . . . hydroelectric plants for power; we opened coal mines, we constructed houses, towns, hospitals, schools and recreation grounds [and] gave a living directly and indirectly to over 100,000 Chinese, Shans and Indians of many dialects—a better living than ever before in their lives. . . ."

Hoover himself did not believe in low wages as a means of building profits. He much preferred labor productivity and management efficiency. Once, for example, when he noted that a supervisor of a Bewick and Moreing mine in South Africa was importing cheap Chinese labor to save costs, he argued against the practice. "I did not believe in it," he bluntly said, and made a short statement before the Transvaal Chamber of Commerce contending that cheap labor was not economical, citing lesser costs per ton in Australia and the United States where labor was better paid. An extension of this labor-management philosophy appeared in *Principles of Mining,* a book he published in 1909.

By this time his earnings had risen to more than $100,000 a year. It seemed he could do whatever he pleased at Bewick and Moreing.

He did, but in a way which dismayed his superiors. After seven years with the firm, the American engineer resigned his partnership to strike out on his own. They begged him to stay and even offered him a larger interest in the company. Hoover declined firmly but politely. He had his reasons.

First of all, he wanted to establish a home in the United States and give his children an American education. Then, too, he and Lou were tired of living out of steamer trunks. They wished to spend more time with friends and family. He had still another thought, the possibility that someday he might be in a position to render a public service to his country.

Hoover left Bewick and Moreing on the best of terms. He was, as a matter of fact, named general manager of the Burma mines, a post he kept while still heading his own company.

For the next six years, from 1908 to 1914, the name Herbert Hoover became synonymous with mining excellence. His firm supervised projects all over the world, including mines in Russia, Australia, Egypt, Italy, Belgium and Burma. He maintained offices in half a dozen European capitals. His staff was made up of the best engineering minds of the times; his own brother, Tad, became one of his ablest assistants.

The very nature of Hoover's work took him all over the world again, though on shorter tours of duty. Lou, for the most part, stayed at home with the two boys, who were both in school, or they traveled with him during the long summer vacations. By 1912 the family had two homes: a cottage near Stanford, California, and a charming old townhouse in London which served as their European headquarters.

During these years, the Hoovers engaged in a unique husband-wife project, the translation of a Latin book on mining and smelting called *De re metallica.* Written originally by Georgius Agricola in 1550, it was the first work to be published on the subject since the Roman period. But since it was written in low Latin, a form understood by few scholars, and because the technology of the Middle Ages had been largely lost, its significance had not yet reached the mining profession.

It was Lou Hoover, an excellent Latin scholar, who suggested they try their hand at the translation. The couple carried on a joint effort for several years, with Lou delving into the text while Hoover tried to duplicate Agricola's experiments wherever he happened to be, either at his small laboratory at home or in one of his mining facilities in the field. Many of the letters they exchanged were long accounts of what each had discovered in Agricola's original text. The book was finally published in 1912 for private circulation among their friends and has since become a valuable collector's item.

In spite of his busy schedule, Herbert Hoover found time to give a series of lectures on his specialty at Stanford. He was also named a trustee of the University in 1912, one of the youngest ever to serve in that capacity.

His residency in the United States finally enabled him to take part in politics that year. He spoke up for Theodore Roosevelt in the presidential elections of 1912 and warmly supported the latter's ill-fated Bull Moose party, which had broken away from the conservative Republican wing headed by William Howard Taft. Both, of course, ran against Woodrow Wilson, the former college president who went to the White House in 1912, due largely to the split in the Republican ranks.

Hoover was a respected man of wealth before his fortieth birthday, actually a millionaire several times over. But he lived quietly, without ostentation, a reserved, portly figure, keenly competent in his profession and painfully shy in all public appearances. In the banking houses and board rooms he invariably appeared in a dark double-breasted suit. The stiff, high-collared shirt he wore in summer and winter became his distinguishing trademark, though at a mining site he donned the baggy coveralls and hard helmets of his profession. But given a few hours off, Herbert Hoover would jump into a pair of hip boots, grab a fishing pole and, pipe in mouth, contentedly cast into the nearest stream. The Bill of Rights, he jokingly once remarked, was based on life, liberty and the pursuit of fish.

But the peace and plenty that he and many others in the world enjoyed came to an abrupt end on June 28, 1914. On that date a group of revolutionary students in the little-known city of Sarajevo, in the equally obscure country of Bosnia, assassinated the Archduke Ferdinand of Austria and thereby unleashed the torrents of a conflict that was soon to engulf Europe and, eventually, the United States.

FIVE

A MONTH AFTER THE ARCHDUKE WAS SHOT DOWN, Austria-Hungary declared war on Serbia, ostensibly for harboring the terrorists who fired the fatal bullet. Russia then went to the aid of her little ally, which promptly brought Germany into the war against the Tzar. France was the next to feel the German boot, and when the Kaiser's Imperial armies marched through Belgium to get at France, England was drawn into the conflict. All this happened between July 28 and August 4, 1914.

The Hoovers, including the eleven-year-old Herbert, Jr., and seven-year-old Allan, were in England that summer. They watched anxiously as tension built day by day through July. Herbert Hoover had to remain in London until the last of his field engineers on the continent could be brought back to safety and paid off. Time enough to go home then.

But the booming guns of August put an end to such hopes. Hoover salvaged what he could of his European operations which, in the summer of 1914, extended from Belgium to the Russian Urals. Just before England's declaration of war he drew enough cash from the bank to meet his payroll.

It was well he did. As soon as hostilities broke out British banks refused to extend credit or even cash checks. Meantime refugees from the continent poured into London. Hotels were jammed. Food suddenly became scarce; cash even scarcer.

Hoover hurried to his office on that first Monday in August, anxious to square his accounts. He had hardly counted out his payroll when he received an urgent call from Robert Skinner, the American Consul General in London. "I'm swamped," the official pleaded. "My office is jammed with American tourists trying to raise cash. Have you any money we can borrow for a week or so until this emergency blows over?"

Hoover had a few hundred pounds beyond his staff needs. He could hardly deny his countrymen in time of need. "Tell your people to line 'em up," he replied. "I'll be over in a few minutes."

He hurried through streets, dodging columns of troops on the march. Flags, shouts and brass bands filled the squares of London. Everywhere he felt the tension of a world at war. Hoover entered the bedlam of the American Consulate, normally the most sedate of offices.

"Small checks only!" he announced briskly. "We'll cash checks only up to five pounds!" Then he took another look at the long lines of worried tourists. His money supply wouldn't last an hour. A few urgent phone calls to business associates quickly raised additional funds, all lent out under Hoover's personal signature.

Word of the engineer's prompt action reached the American Embassy, where Walter Hines Page, the United States envoy, was doing his best to deal with still more waves of Americans besieging his headquarters. "Call Hoover!" he said to an aide. "Ask him to reserve some cash for us! Better still, I'll go see him myself!" The ambassador plunged into the crowded streets. It would have been impossible to drive a car through the throngs that filled Grosvenor Square.

In a few hours a semblance of sanity had been restored under Hoover's calm direction. By the end of the day nearly a thousand stranded Americans had at least enough cash to see them through for the next couple of days. But what to do about feeding and housing them, and arranging for their eventual return home?

Ambassador Page and Consul General Skinner looked at one another, then at the unperturbed figure of the shirt-sleeved engineer bringing order out of chaos. They both nodded in agreement. Here was their man, delivered to their doorstep. That night, over a late dinner, they put the question to Herbert Hoover. Would he direct the American refugee program, at least on a temporary basis?

Hoover agreed. At any rate, there was very little he could do about his own affairs for the time being.

The Savoy Hotel in London donated working space. Five of his own engineers left their blueprints to man emergency desks. Mrs. Hoover joined the group. "The Chief," as Hoover had been affectionately called by his staff, now became, in reality, the chief of rescue operations.

For the next six weeks his volunteer organization went

on a round-the-clock basis. Emergency housing and mess halls were set up for stranded tourists, clothing distributed to those who had fled Europe with only what they were wearing on their backs. Passage on neutral ships was obtained and American schoolchildren on the continent were safely retrieved through the war zones. In all, 120,000 Americans were returned home and more than $1,500,000 disbursed, of which all but $300 was eventually recovered.

When word reached the United States about the identity of the man directing relief efforts in London, eyebrows went up in surprise. "Herbert Hoover? Who's he?"

"Some sort of mining engineer, I think."

This was the first time the American public became aware of his name, if only in a limited way.

Among the last to leave London that September were Mrs. Hoover and her two boys. "I'll join you in California," the father promised them at dockside. "Just as soon as the situation clears up."

The situation, however, grew worse. The armies of the Kaiser tightened their hold on Belgium and advanced into France. The Allies, in retaliation, threw a naval blockade around the ports of the North Atlantic. If Germany could not be battered into submission, she would be starved into it.

The strategy proved cruelly effective. The first to feel the pinch were 7,500,000 helpless Belgian civilians caught in the squeeze of occupation from within and blockade from without. Food shipments into a nation that normally imported eighty percent of her needs were reduced to a trickle. To the grim specter of war was now added the quiet terror of starvation.

Businessmen escaping Belgium, among them some of Hoover's associates, urged the Allies to lift the blockade long enough to send in food supplies. Britain and France refused, insisting that it was the duty of the occupying forces to feed the civilian population. Besides, they had every reason to suspect that the Germans would confiscate the food for their own use and thus prolong the war.

Meantime, the Belgians tightened their belts. The eyes of their children grew haunted. The fall harvest, pitifully small, was immediately impounded by the enemy.

The worried Allies conferred, then approached Ambassador Page. Would he ask Herbert Hoover to take charge of another humanitarian effort, at least until the harvest next fall? The war would surely be over by then!

"I will need to think about it, Mr. Page," Hoover replied. Then he left for his London townhouse, to ponder his problem.

For three days and nights Hoover struggled with his conscience. On the one hand, there were millions of war victims in desperate need of help. An undeniable fact. On the other hand, he had to consider his career, his staff and his clients.

Hoover might have slipped into a convenient decision: stick to engineering and help the Allied war effort. Surely his mines, with their treasures of zinc and lead and copper, would be of enormous assistance to England and France. Being a realist, he knew that his holdings would probably make him a millionaire many, many times over, particularly if the conflict dragged on for any length of time. However, Herbert Hoover was also a Quaker. War and its wanton destruction repelled him. Yet, how could he give up a career to which he had devoted a lifetime?

His soul searching was poignantly described by Will Irwin, who was, at the time, a war correspondent in London for *The Saturday Evening Post.* A house guest of Hoover's, he wrote that he heard his host pace the floor for three nights, obviously struggling with a dilemma. Finally, on the morning of the fourth day, Irwin recalled, Hoover came down to breakfast, poured out a cup of coffee, then looked up in grim satisfaction. "Well, let the fortune go to hell!"

Never one to fall back on strong language, though he had heard his share in his lifetime, Hoover now used it to underline his moment of truth. "My engineering career," he later admitted, "was over forever. I was on the slippery road of public life."

He resigned from all his mining interests save the Burma project, which he eventually disposed of in 1918. Nor would he accept any salary as head of the Commission for the Relief of Belgium, as the Allied effort was called. Unthinkable that anyone should profit from the misfortune of others. For the next few years—indeed, throughout his long career as a public servant at home and abroad—Herbert Hoover relied chiefly on his own substantial fortune for his livelihood.

He attacked his new post as if it were a gigantic problem in engineering. Food supplies had to be gathered, crated, stored, shipped and distributed. Offices had to be established in the field and responsible men put in charge. And, of course, money had to be raised, more money than was ever required for a mining project!

Before taking leadership of the Commission for the Relief of Belgium, or the CRB, Hoover had insisted that he have absolute command of the operation. Assured of that, he set up a board of directors with himself as chairman, including five of his best engineers, as well as two newspapermen, one of whom was Will Irwin. He established headquarters in Brussels, London and New York, with other branches throughout Europe, including offices in two neutral nations, Spain and Holland. To himself he assigned the most difficult task of all: raising money and dealing with the foreign ministers of Allied, neutral and enemy nations.

The Chief took one more precaution. He retained a firm of auditors to keep an eagle eye on all CRB income and expenditures so that, when the job was over, he could account for every penny spent by his organization.

Late in 1914, he crossed the English Channel for a first-hand look at the machinery of relief distribution. It was the first of perhaps fifty such crossings through waters sprinkled with mines. His impressions of that initial visit to Belgium remained painfully clear.

"Passing through the frontier from Holland," he wrote in his memoirs, "I had an indescribable feeling of entering a land of imprisonment. Possibly the rather rough search of my person by German guards strengthened that impression. German soldiers stood at every crossroads and every street corner. The depressed, unsmiling faces of the Belgians matched the mood of the dreary winter landscapes. There were no children at play . . ."

The job proved to be far more complicated than even he had imagined. Ten million people, including several millions in northern France, had to be fed a minimum of 1800 calories a day. Hoover estimated the cost at about $12 million a month, only a bit less than the amount the CRB then had in bank credits. Obviously, he would have to get financial support from the various governments involved, which proved to be easier said than done, as Hoover soon found out.

Spokesmen for the British Cabinet told him that England was opposed to the whole idea of feeding the Belgians. "The food will only wind up in German hands!" they insisted. Lord Kitchener, the Minister of War, and Winston Churchill, then the First Lord of the Admiralty, led the attack. Churchill's own ministry, perversely enough, filed charges to the effect that Herbert Hoover was a German spy bringing aid and comfort to the enemy by delivering food to occupied Belgium!

"After tedious hearings," Hoover explained, "we were exonerated and eulogized."

He then turned his attention to Germany. Obviously, for the relief program to succeed, cooperation was essential from that quarter. Much to his surprise, the Germans agreed not to confiscate food supplies or interfere with the CRB staff in occupied territory. They also agreed not to attack marked supply ships on the high seas; at the time Germany's most effective weapon against the Allies was her submarines. Furthermore, German officials arranged a trade pact with the United States which would assure some $50 to $100 million worth of food for the Belgians provided inflation, a constant threat, did not wipe out the currency of the Reichsbank.

In spite of these assurances, Hoover left Berlin with misgivings. "Every one of the officials was in uniform of some sort," he said, "all cogs in a military machine. Their attitudes were military. Their minds were military. There was something indescribably automatic and inhuman about their actions and thinking. For the first time in modern history a nation was incorporating its full human power into its striking strength."

He returned to England that winter firmly convinced that the war could not possibly end by spring, as the Allies hoped. In fact, Hoover believed that the war had not yet really begun.

The harsh realities of famine eventually melted Allied hearts and purse strings. In February 1915, Britain promised the CRB about $5,000,000 a month; a few weeks later France donated a similar amount. In the entire course of the war, which was to last for nearly four more years, the commission spent nearly $928 million. With the exception of about $4,000,000 for overhead expenses —less than one half of one percent—every penny went for food and relief supplies. Of the above total, more than one third, or about $386 million, came from the United States government. In all, more than five million tons of food, clothing and medical supplies were distributed by the CRB.

Of greater significance was the human story behind these statistics. A "Hoover cookie," a nutritional cracker developed by the CRB director and Dr. William Lucas of California, supplied essential food elements for a daily soup lunch for over 2,500,000 children in Belgium. Other supplies flowed out to the countryside. Those who could pay for the food did so; those who were destitute were fed without cost. Mass hunger, if not wiped out, was at least allayed, and the Belgian population had the dubious satisfaction of knowing that while shellfire might destroy them, starvation would not.

Hoover's selfless example of service motivated others. Men left well-paying jobs to work for CRB, often for expenses only. Volunteers in Belgium and northern France organized their own soup kitchens and distribution centers. Charities in America poured millions of dollars into the cause, as did fund-raising committees throughout Europe.

During these difficult years, Mrs. Hoover was constantly at his side. She joined him in London after placing her two sons in a California boarding school. Hoover had, on the whole, much to be grateful for.

And much over which to be disturbed. Some of the CRB supply ships fell prey to German U-boats, in spite of earlier assurances to the contrary. Then, on May 7, 1915, the *Lusitania* was torpedoed. Twelve hundred lives were lost, including 124 Americans. How much longer, he wondered, could the United States stay out of the war?

Public sentiment at home, almost solidly against intervention at first, now began to swing the other way. However, a strong group in the Wilson administration, led by Secretary of State William Jennings Bryan, a pacifist, and Senator Henry Cabot Lodge, were doing their utmost to keep the United States out of foreign entanglements. Senator Lodge, the same man who had beaten the drum for U.S. military intervention in Cuba nearly twenty years before, brought the CRB under his investigative eye. He insisted that American citizens, Hoover in particular, had no business dealing with foreign governments. His attitude seemed to be; let the belligerents feed the hungry!

Pressure from Lodge eventually forced the CRB director to return to America in May, 1915, for a "clear-the-air" conference with President Wilson. A vote of confidence from the White House was essential and Hoover meant to get it.

The two men met face to face for the first time that spring. Each already had a great respect for the other. Wilson admired Hoover for his selfless work for the CRB, while Hoover returned the compliment because of the President's determined, though fruitless, attempts to bring peace to Europe. The relief director knew that many problems weighed heavily on the President. But could he spare a few moments to help him with his Congressional critics, Senator Lodge in particular?

Wilson listened, his long thin face nodding in sympathy. No friend of the senator's (he hated Lodge, Hoover remembered), Wilson finally agreed to issue a supporting statement for the CRB which Hoover had had the foresight to prepare. The Lodge burr, for the moment, was removed, thanks to a joint effort by a Democratic President and a humanitarian who also happened to be a lifelong Republican.

They met again under even more critical conditions nearly two years later. In March 1917, when the United States' entry into the war seemed imminent due to German provocation, Hoover was hurriedly recalled to Washington. What role, President Wilson wanted to know, would food play in the event America joined with the Allies?

Hoover told him that second only to military action, food was the dominant factor.

Wilson had another question. Would America's entry mean the end of Belgian relief?

"Not necessarily," came the reply. "I hope we can transfer our guardianship to the neutral Dutch and Spanish."

Hoover then returned to London. Two days later, on April 7, 1917, the news flashed around the world—America had joined the war on the side of the Allies.

The following morning Ambassador Page handed the CRB director an urgent cable from President Wilson: "Can you return and take charge of the wartime food organization for the United States?"

Hoover agreed but attached two conditions. First, he insisted on remaining as director of Belgian relief; second, he wanted no salary for his services. "I believed," he explained later, "that the position would carry more moral leadership if I were a volunteer alongside my countrymen at war."

Washington in the summer of 1917 was hot and humid, just as it is every summer. Add the compelling urgency of wartime and it became a three-ring circus, only not as well organized, as Hoover soon learned.

But there was compensation for the new United States Food Administrator, his official title in the new job. Herbert, Jr., and Allan, now fourteen and ten, joined their parents. This was the first time the family had been together for any length of time since the outbreak of the war in Europe. It was a comfort for Hoover to return to his family after an exhausting fourteen-hour day in the office.

Comfort, too, came from old friends who flocked to Washington to help tackle the enormous job of keeping American troops supplied with food. Many of them, like their chief, accepted no salary other than expenses.

Hoover conducted his agency with a firm hand, without divided responsibility, and with himself in full command. He felt there must be a single head to the food problem and that his authority must cover every phase of food administration from the soil to the stomach.

The "soil to the stomach" program, as he so inelegantly but aptly put it, was based on a decentralized system of volunteer citizen cooperation on all levels: producers, processors, retailers and consumers. Regional, state and local boards, serving without pay, kept a sharp eye on guidelines issued by his agency. In addition, Hoover established price guarantees on the wholesale level as opposed to retail price controls. His philosophy was that if America grew enough food, and if farmers and other basic producers got a decent return for their output, there would be no need for rationing, and no need for regulatory control from Washington and, consequently, no black market.

In 1917–18, few argued with Hoover's direction of the U.S. Food Administration program. Made aware that "food will win the war," Americans willingly accepted meatless days and sweetless days and family garden patches. The nation became "Hooverized" with a minimum of grumbling.

"Go back to simple foods, simple clothes and simple pleasures," Hoover urged his fellow citizens. "Pray hard, work hard, sleep hard and play hard. Do it all courageously and cheerfully. We have a victory to win."

The victory was won with the signing of the Armistice on November 11, 1918.

If the cost of the conflict to the United States was great in terms of lives and money, it was a catastrophe to the Allies and their conquered enemies. Many of their towns and cities were destroyed, their transportation lines shattered, their economic systems ruined, their populations decimated. Some were riven by internal strife, as in Russia, where the Bolshevik Revolution under Lenin had wrested control from the moderate Kerensky regime which had, in turn, succeeded the deposed Tzar in 1917.

Behind all that turmoil Hoover recognized an old

enemy—hunger. At war's end, he estimated that all of Europe—Allies, neutrals, enemies—twenty-six nations—were faced with some shortage of food. He urged a gigantic effort to save Europe from "the flames of starvation, pestilence, revolution. If the furnace of famine continues to burn no peace can be made. And from its aftermath, no hope of a better world to come."

President Wilson agreed. Six days after the Armistice went into effect, Herbert Hoover was on his way back to Europe. The somber forty-four-year-old Quaker now had a third title, Director of the American Relief Administration in Europe.

SIX

HERBERT HOOVER ARRIVED IN PARIS WITH MIXED emotions.

The most dreadful war in history had ended, leaving behind a toll of over thirty million dead, maimed and missing. Now was the time to heal wounds, feed the hungry, rebuild cities and so plan the future that never again would nation take up arms against nation.

Liberty, freedom and democracy, Hoover noted, were the watchwords of the day. But with the best of intentions, these watchwords, in his opinion, were already being undermined at home and abroad.

Wilson's plan for a League of Nations, the last of his Fourteen Points for a postwar world at peace, was under attack in Congress. Strong opposition to it was raised by Senators Henry Cabot Lodge, William Borah and Hiram Johnson, who warned they would never vote for an international body which they felt would compromise the sovereignty of the United States. Hoover, on the other hand, had warmly supported the League in the congressional elections of 1918. "I considered it my duty," he explained, "to support Congressmen who were loyal to Wilson's objectives whether Republicans or Democrats. An adverse vote would greatly weaken Mr. Wilson's hand in making the peace. It did," he laconically concluded when the Democrats that fall lost their grip in both houses. Hoover was severely criticized for his bipartisan stand by certain Republican politicians even though he had been a party faithful all his life.

Hoover also was smarting under another attack. Last summer, feeling it necessary to keep wartime profits at a reasonable level, he had recommended an excise profits tax, a move which won him no friends in some quarters.

But most of all he was troubled by the self-centered attitudes of the victorious European Allies as represented by Georges Clemenceau, the "Old Tiger" of France, Lloyd George of England and Vittorio Orlando of Italy. Together with Woodrow Wilson, who headed the American delegation, they made up the Big Four, or the Supreme Council which met in Paris to decide the fate of postwar Europe. Spokesmen for twenty other countries, more or less—nations and boundaries were changing in those days with the rapidity of summer clouds—also sat in on the deliberations.

When President Wilson arrived in the French capital on December 15, 1918, he asked Hoover what he thought of the general situation in Europe. "The people are facing a famine worse than the Thirty Years' War," the ARA director replied. As for politics, he saw little tolerance and generosity among the winners, and a good deal of greed, power and hate. The idealistic Wilson simply would not believe these words; later he admitted, sorrowfully, they were more right than wrong.

Among the Big Four's first acts was to put Herbert

Hoover in charge of the rehabilitation program on the continent, one of their few unanimous decisions. In other matters they were at loggerheads, principally over three issues.

First, the European ministers insisted that America place all her resources into a common pool. The general idea, Hoover guessed, correctly as it turned out, was that through the power of American bunker-coal, food, shipping and credit, they could force the neutral world to contribute to the rehabilitation of the Allies themselves. The United States delegation rejected the plan in Paris as they had done earlier in Washington.

Second, the European heads of state were determined to make America reduce the price of her foodstuffs. This Wilson could not do. Staggering wheat and pork surpluses had been built up at home, all on the firm promise of price supports for future delivery. To do so would have pulled the rug out from under America's agricultural economy.

And third, they insisted on maintaining, and even extending, the naval blockade on neutral and liberated countries until the peace treaty was signed. Hoover rightly saw this as a power play to force Germany and Austria to accept terms imposed on them by England and France.

With the Big Four bogged down in interminable bickering, the ARA director took matters into his own hands. Since starvation does not await the outcome of power politics, Hoover decided to attend to the famine and reconstruction and let the power politicians work all by themselves. He felt the American people did not require the permission of anybody to undertake the second intervention in Europe.

In this he was backed by President Wilson and General John J. Pershing, head of the American Expeditionary Forces. "I shall always be ready to assist in any way," the General told Hoover, then promptly assigned him several thousand Army and Navy men who proceeded to run the blockade to neutral ports. In the face of such determined action, the British, French and Italian ministers offered only token resistance. They were less lenient with Germany and Austria, with whom they were still technically at war. Hoover pleaded for the lifting of that blockade without success. Even so, he managed, in time, to negotiate trade agreements which sent German gold to the United States in exchange for desperately needed food.

By the end of the year, a hundred American ships were shuttling across the Atlantic. Dumping their cargoes of food in Europe, they returned to America with shiploads of homesick doughboys, then steamed back with more wheat, tinned milk, meat, cocoa, lard and coffee.

The problems which Hoover now faced as ARA director made his former job as Food Administrator seem as simple as running a general store. Getting shipments from ports to inland distribution centers required courage and improvisation. Rail lines were ripped up, bridges destroyed, telegraph lines down. But the engineer was never far below the surface of the humanitarian.

Hoover's technicians soon put together a patchwork transportation system that worked . . . most of the time.

He also had trouble with passports and visas. Since hundreds of ARA supervisors had to travel all over Europe, many on short notice, Hoover persuaded the Supreme Council to issue special ARA passes. These worked like magic. While diplomats and businessmen often cooled their heels at border crossings, ARA men were waved on by smiling border guards. Their presence, after all, meant food, a language any man could understand.

There were other difficulties; inflation, the complexities of foreign exchange, censorship, pestilence, strikes, riots, revolutions and, always, the frantic search for money to keep the relief pipelines flowing. Will Irwin, watching his chief in action, made a cogent observation: "I think of Hoover as a chessmaster, playing twenty games at once, most of them blindfolded."

The chessmaster played out his string. Over the next eighteen months he estimated that fourteen to sixteen million children were saved from famine. Others insisted the figure was closer to twenty million.

The food tonnage was more accurately measured. About twenty-seven million tons of food were distributed by the ARA during this period, as well as many more million tons of coal, clothing and medical supplies.

Behind Hoover's humanitarian actions there were at least two realistic factors: the American surplus at home and the threat of Communism in Europe. In supplying food to Europe, he was safeguarding the farm and food industries of the United States. It was a case of economic needs at home and humanitarian needs abroad coinciding. Hoover also believed that people who were fed properly and who had homes and jobs could better resist the lure of the Bolsheviks, as Communists were known at the time.

Hoover normally took his agency's difficulties in stride, rarely losing his temper. But one time, when he was in the midst of a vast relief program for Soviet Russia during that country's great famine of 1921, an indignant American woman questioned his tactics. "But helping Bolsheviks!" she gasped. "Isn't that carrying charity too far?" This was too much for Hoover.

"Madame!" His voice shook with anger. "Hunger is hunger, whether at home or abroad! People shall be fed, whatever their politics!"

The Hoover mission to Russia, which was organized after his return to the United States, sent 150 shiploads of food in 1921–1922. Its medical teams inoculated millions of men, women and children against typhus, smallpox and cholera. In partial return, the Soviets released more than a hundred American prisoners, an agreement Hoover worked out even before the first relief supplies arrived on Russian soil.

There was one more response to this episode. Hoover received a letter from Maxim Gorki, the great Russian novelist who had originally appealed for the American aid. "In all the history of human suffering," he wrote, "I know of nothing more trying to the souls of men than the events through which the Russian people are passing, and in the history of practical humanitarianism I know of no accomplishment which in terms of magnitude and generosity can be compared to the relief you have actually accomplished. . . . Your help will be inscribed in history . . . and will long remain in the memory of millions of Russian children whom you saved from death."

That recurring theme, children, cropped up again and again in Herbert Hoover's life. His first thought in Belgian relief was to feed the children. Later on, in Russia, the plight of boys and girls caught in famine wiped out all political barriers. His repeated insistence on feeding the young people of enemy nations frequently brought criticism raining down upon his head, but the Quaker held firm to his ideals. The orphan boy from West Branch, Iowa, had indeed become the symbolic father to millions of homeless and hungry children.

In Poland some fifty thousand boys and girls dressed in rags paraded before Hoover in the summer of 1919 when he paid a brief visit to that country. Their smiles and cheers and glowing eyes touched even battle-hardened soldiers. General Henrys, head of the French Military Mission, who was at the parade, turned to Hoover with tears in his eyes and said: "There has never been a review of honor in all history which I would prefer for myself to that which has been given you today."

At a reception that evening, more praise was heaped on the American Quaker, this time by Ignace Jan Paderewski, the world-famous pianist and Poland's first postwar Premier. Hoover's response was nostalgically brief. "I need only remind the Premier," he said, "of the concert he gave at Stanford when I was a student there. I still owe him four hundred dollars for that appearance."

The cheers of the audience wiped out that debt then and there.

Although not a member of the United States Peace Commission in Paris, Hoover conferred with its members almost daily, sometimes hourly, as he remembered it. And with good reason, for he and his staff knew every back alley and village in Europe. Everything he had learned about conditions in other countries he now made available to President Wilson, who was desperately trying to get his peace program approved by the other Allies.

But the "new order" of America never had a chance against the "old order" of Europe. Britain, France and Italy only gave lip service to Wilson's proposals. "Open covenants, openly arrived at," the first of his Fourteen Points, was turned into an ill-concealed joke as the vengeance-driven Clemenceau, the adroit Lloyd George and the suave Orlando revived secret agreements made during the war. As for the League of Nations, the last of the Fourteen Points, it was treated as a bit of high-flown idealism.

In the meantime, the peace conference sputtered along as the entire world waited and wondered.

Then, on the night of May 7, 1919, Hoover was

roused from a deep sleep by a messenger who handed him an advance copy of the German peace treaty marked "personal and confidential." The ARA director shook himself awake and read the document on the spot. His heart grew heavier with each clause. It was a treaty based on revenge. If the Allies could not "Hang the Kaiser!" as Lloyd George had demanded, then they could certainly bring the German nation to its knees. Hoover was convinced this was a mistake and carried with it built-in conditions of a later conflict.

Others shared his views, among them Jan Christian Smuts of South Africa, John Maynard Keynes of England and Vance McCormick, the American chairman of the War Trades Board. Individually and collectively, they tried to persuade the Big Four to soften the treaty. Lloyd George made a few minor adjustments, but not enough to suit Keynes, who quit the British delegation in protest. Colonel House, Wilson's adviser, also left in sharp disagreement.

Hoover conferred with Wilson several times on this subject and even sent him a lengthy memorandum pointing to economic fallacies in the treaty. He argued that if the United States demanded reparations of coal from Germany, while taking away her coal fields in Saar and Silesia, as the treaty provided, it would reduce her supply to little more than household consumption, leaving nothing for railways, utilities and manufacture.

His last meeting with Wilson turned out badly when, by his own admission, Hoover used overvigorous words. The President, he recalled, "flashed angrily at these expressions as . . . personal attacks," the last thing in the world the gentle Quaker intended. But he knew the Chief Executive was tired and sick. He had, as a matter of fact, been through a siege of the flu. It wasn't until later that a member of the President's staff told Hoover that Wilson had actually suffered a mild thrombosis that summer. At any rate, the relationship between the two men, which had begun so promisingly four years before, came to an unhappy end in the summer of 1919.

"Other than a formal goodbye at the railway station," Hoover remembered, "I never saw him again while he was in the Presidency."

His efforts to moderate the German treaty might have gone unnoticed except for John Maynard Keynes. "Mr. Hoover," the British economist wrote, "was the only man to emerge from the ordeal of Paris with an enhanced reputation." He compared the American to "a weary titan . . . an exhausted prizefighter . . . his eyes fixed on the true and essential facts of the European situation."

Soon after the peace treaty was signed in the Versailles Palace Hall of Mirrors on June 28, 1919, Hoover fixed his eyes on home. His relief job in Europe was just about over. The fall harvests would soon be coming in. It was time for the American Relief Administration to haul in its reins.

And time for Herbert Hoover to get back to his profession. After all, he told himself, he was a mining engineer, not a politician. And he was still in his middle forties, not too late to get back into the swing of things.

SEVEN

THE HOOVERS SPENT THE WHOLE OF THE NEXT September on a fishing trip in California.

Herbert, Jr., now a strapping seventeen, and his brother Allan, four years younger, took off to the trout streams with their father. Mrs. Hoover, meanwhile, worked over plans for a larger home to be built near the campus of Stanford University. It was the first time in years that the family had a chance to rest in isolation.

But the pressure of public service soon caught up with Herbert Hoover. An urgent appeal reached him from ARA headquarters in New York. The postwar harvest in Europe had fallen far below expectations, it said. Production was sporadic due to revolt and unrest. Hunger again was stalking the continent. Would he consider a temporary assignment to get relief machinery rolling once again?

This time Hoover left the decision to his family. "We need not go overseas," he told them. "I am asked only to tour the country, make speeches, raise money and coordinate a children's relief council in New York. What do you say?"

Next week they were on their way East, their fishing gear packed, their house plans postponed, the boys' school records transferred to New York. Mrs. Hoover and the two boys lived in an apartment while the head of the family traveled about the country.

"I adopted a Pullman berth as my eternal home," Hoover said of this period.

Herbert Hoover's frequent public appearances on behalf of the Children's Relief Council made his name and face better known throughout the country. Inevitably politics caught up with him. His name appeared on the first four presidential ballots in the 1920 National Republican Convention. The reluctant candidate refused to put much stock in his nomination and was relieved when delegates chose Senator Warren Harding of Ohio, with Calvin Coolidge, the Massachusetts governor, as his running mate.

But if the Republicans didn't want him for the top spot that year, the Democrats did. Here was a man, they knew, who had once supported a Democratic President, and could now command respect among voters of both major parties. Hoover-for-President clubs appeared in spite of his protest that he had been a registered Republican since his twenty-first birthday. Even so, his name popped up on several Democratic primaries. However, it never got to the convention floor.

The Democrats that year nominated James M. Cox, Governor of Ohio, as their standard bearer with young Franklin Delano Roosevelt, who had served as Wilson's Assistant Secretary of the Navy, in the second slot.

Voters could not have had a clearer choice in 1920.

The Democratic platform carried a strong endorsement of the League of Nations. The Republicans did not, in spite of the fact that Warren Harding had once supported the idea as a senator. In the campaign he vacillated on that particular issue, carrying "water on both shoulders," as Hoover put it.

Hoover felt his party's attitude was short-sighted. The Republicans avoided the deeper issues in their campaign, and concentrated on a platform of restoring "normalcy" to the country. It seemed to be just what the people wanted, for the Republicans won by a landslide. Subsequently, the United States Senate effectively blocked America's participation in the League.

Following the 1920 elections, the Hoover family once more cast longing eyes toward California. "Time we went back to fishing," the boys pleaded. Time for the father to open his long-awaited engineering office in San Francisco. Former clients were clamoring for his services.

But Hoover hadn't counted on the strong impression he had made on Harding, in spite of the differences between them. For his part, the President-elect knew the engineer to be a man of unquestioned ability; he meant to have him on his team. Accordingly Harding made him a flattering offer: he could either become his Secretary of the Interior or Secretary of Commerce.

Surprised, and pleased, Hoover gave the proposal hard thought, hard because he had just been approached a few weeks before by the Guggenheim brothers, then the largest mining firm in the world. They had offered him a salary many times over what he could earn in government service.

After days of deliberation, reminiscent of his Belgian Relief decision, Quaker conscience prevailed over monetary gain. Hoover chose the post of Secretary of Commerce. After all, his own country badly needed economic development. And so the family moved once more, this time to Washington, D.C., where Herbert Hoover was confirmed by the Senate as Harding's Secretary of Commerce on March 4, 1921.

At this point, the new Secretary made his usual stipulation before taking public office. He would accept no salary in a government post. When told that this was impossible, that it would upset budgetary procedures, Hoover simply used his cabinet salary to hire several assistants at his own expense.

Furthermore, he insisted that he must have a voice on major policies involving labor, since he had no belief that commerce and industry could progress unless labor advanced with them. Secretary of Labor James J. Davis offered no objection. Labor, in those days, needed all the help it could get.

Upon taking office, the new Secretary was told he had one of the softest jobs in government, one that wouldn't take more than two hours a day. Since the Commerce Department's duties included supervision of the Bureau of Fisheries and the Bureau of Navigation, he was advised that all he had to do was "put the fish to bed and turn up the lights up and down the coast."

Hoover's response was a curt nod. He hadn't joined the Cabinet, he said, just to put fish to bed and turn up the lights. *Or* to work two hours a day. There must be something more to the job.

He began to dig. He discovered, much to his professional delight, that his department was also responsible for the Bureau of the Census, domestic and international business regulations, inland waterways, government purchasing practices, the development of trade associations and two infant, and, at the time, lightly regarded, industries, commercial aviation and radio broadcasting.

Like any other good engineer, Herbert Hoover started with basic fundamentals. He eliminated purely political jobholders and replaced them with qualified civil service personnel, regardless of party affiliation. He brought new life to the Bureau of the Census and soon transformed it from merely a population-counting agency into the greatest fact-finding institution in the world. He expanded the Bureau of Fisheries and drew up a vast program for the utilization of inland waterways, including the Mississippi River, the Colorado River Basin and the Columbia River complex in the Northwest.

He also brought the Bureau of Mines into his department. A former mucker, Hoover astounded technicians with his knowledge of mining. Many of today's health and safety regulations in the mines are due to his concern for miners.

The new Secretary found still more challenges: he encouraged the formation of trade associations among American businessmen. Where there had been only a handful when he first took office, there were more than two thousand at the end of his two terms as Commerce chief. His sense of order and his knowledge of production problems led him to suggest standard sizes for the manufacture of automobile wheels, building bricks, nuts, bolts and lumber components. When businessmen saw they could cut costs and eliminate waste through standardization, they readily accepted his recommendations.

Perhaps no one was more responsible for the orderly development of commercial aviation and radio, and ultimately television, than Secretary Hoover. Today, both are multibillion-dollar industries and owe much of their growth to the support he gave them in the early 1920s.

In 1922 he convened the first radio conference between industry and government, which established a set of rules for the proper use and distribution of wave lengths. When his voluntary guidelines were broken by a few station operators, among them evangelist Aimee Semple McPherson, the government stepped in with more stringent regulations. This was the basis of the Federal Communications Commission, established in 1934, which today regulates all domestic radio and television broadcasting.

His department gave a similar start to commercial aviation. In 1922, at a time when Congress was indifferent to the industry—many thought aviation had no use beyond the military—Hoover called a meeting of manufacturers, engineers and pilots. This group studied the commercial possibilities for air mail, passenger travel and transport. In subsequent meetings it drew up flight regulations which, together with Hoover's plans for a Bureau of Aviation, eventually grew into the Civil Aeronautics Board, formalized in 1940.

But the cabinet post was not without its difficulties. Hoover's chief critic in the Harding administration was Henry W. Wallace, the Secretary of Agriculture, father of Henry A. Wallace, who held the same post many years later under Franklin D. Roosevelt. The two Secretaries disagreed over departmental functions. Hoover felt that Agriculture should limit itself to telling farmers what to grow and how to grow it and leave the disposal of produce up to Commerce.

The elder Wallace strongly resisted this apparent intrusion. He bristled at the thought of the American farmer taking orders from a business-oriented agency. As a matter of record, Wallace had been highly critical of Hoover during the latter's service as War Food Administrator. In 1920 he wrote that Hoover's dealings "with hog and milk and beef producers gave evidence of a mental bias which causes farmers to thoroughly distrust him. They look upon him as a typical autocrat of big business." This was one of the earliest attacks on Hoover for his business affiliations. It was not to be the last.

The feud between them continued until Wallace's death in 1924. He was then replaced by W. M. Jardine, one of whose first acts, Hoover wrote, "was to pay tribute to the Department of Commerce for its service to farmers. He established at once full cooperation with us."

Hoover's knowledge and wide background won him the admiration of his President very early in office. "Hoover," Harding once remarked in one of his typically earthy evaluations, "is the damnedest smartest man I have ever met."

The contrast between Harding and Hoover intrigued political observers. The President was a florid, gray-haired crowd-pleaser, no stranger to either smoke-filled rooms or rum-filled companions. A *bon vivant,* he surrounded himself with his "Ohio gang," cronies of his former days as newspaper editor and political roustabout. To Harding's credit, he also chose men of unquestioned ability, among them Charles Evans Hughes as Secretary of State, Andrew Mellon as Secretary of the Treasury, Will Hays as Postmaster General as well as Hoover. But he could not cast off his old ways and old habits. It has been said of Harding that if his skill in statesmanship equaled his skill at poker, he might have become one of the more competent Presidents of the United States.

Hoover himself saw the Chief Executive as a kind of dual personality, whose responsibilities in the White House gave him a real spiritual lift. But, the Secretary concluded, he was not a man with either the experience or the intellectual quality that the position needed.

But Harding had courage. Hoover applauded his actions when the President stood up against the entire steel industry and demanded that it put an end to the twelve-hour work day and the seven-day week. The ammunition for shorter hours was supplied largely by

Hoover himself. The industry eventually complied, though not willingly.

Hoover's record on labor was somewhat spotty, judged by today's standards. As Secretary of Commerce, he supported labor organizations and collective bargaining, but opposed the closed shop (compulsory membership in a union in order to obtain employment) and featherbedding (multiple workers to perform the same job at the same time) as denials of human freedom. He also hailed the American Federation of Labor as a bulwark against socialism. He later described the CIO, organized in 1935, as socialist and Communist-controlled in its early days, though he lived to see the day in 1955 when both groups merged to form the present AFL-CIO.

Hoover recognized and supported labor's right to strike. One morning, in 1922, he learned that Attorney General Harry Daugherty, one of Harding's closest friends, had issued an injunction against railway workers then on strike.

"I was outraged by its obvious transgressions of the most rudimentary rights of the men," Hoover said of the incident. At the next cabinet meeting he bitterly protested Daugherty's action. When Secretary of State Hughes, an eminent jurist, supported the legal points of Hoover's protest, President Harding turned to his Attorney General and demanded an explanation.

Daugherty had none. Harding abruptly instructed him to withdraw those sections of the injunction at once. Daugherty dropped the whole action as quickly as possible. One direct result of Hoover's concern for labor was the formation of the Railway Labor Mediation Board, which he helped organize in 1926.

Antagonism mounted between Hoover and Daugherty. The Attorney General frequently went to poker parties given by the President. Hoover was invited once, disliked the idea of gambling in the White House, and kept out of the game—and out of Daugherty's way.

Meantime, the Secretary of Commerce became more and more concerned as scandal began to touch the Harding administration. One member, Charles Cramer, had committed suicide when a Senate investigation turned up some ugly facts about the Veterans' Bureau. Another, Jesse Smith of the Department of Justice, also took his own life soon after. During this time Harding was exceedingly nervous and distraught, according to Hoover.

In June 1923, Secretary Hoover was traveling in the West when he and his wife received an invitation to accompany the President and his party on a trip to Alaska. "I was naturally surprised," Hoover wrote, "since it was announced that Daugherty and others of his cronies were to be the guests." Nevertheless, they joined the presidential steamship party at Tacoma on July 3, 1923.

Hoover sensed an air of tension as soon as he stepped aboard. Harding insisted on playing bridge every day, stopping only for meals. The Commerce Secretary knew there were meetings to be held, speeches to write, figures to compile. But the President refused to leave the bridge table except to eat or sleep.

After several days at sea, Harding broke his routine

long enough to call Hoover to his cabin. Obviously agitated, he sent the steward out of the room and motioned his Secretary to sit down.

"Tell me, Mr. Secretary"—Harding never used the first-name approach with Hoover—"if you knew of a great scandal in our administration, would you for the good of the country and the party expose it publicly or would you bury it?"

"Publish it," came the prompt reply, "and at least get credit for integrity on your side."

"It could be politically dangerous."

Hoover asked for particulars. Harding told him some of the details that had preceeded Smith's suicide. "I sent for Smith," the President explained. "After a painful session, I told him that I had no choice but to have him arrested in the morning. That night he went home and apparently burned his papers. The rest you know."

"What had Smith been up to?" Hoover asked.

Harding did not answer.

"What relation did Harry Daugherty have to this whole affair?" the Secretary pressed on.

Harding looked up, opened his mouth for a moment, then shook his head. In Hoover's own words: "He abruptly dried up and never raised the question again."

A worried Secretary of Commerce now kept a close watch on his Chief Executive. "He grew more nervous as the trip continued," he remembered. "Despite his natural geniality, he was now obviously forcing gaiety. He sought for excitement from the receptions, parades, and speeches at every port. To the rest of us, these events were at least some relief from the everlasting bridge games."

On the return from Alaska, the party stopped off in Seattle on July 27, 1923. That afternoon, according to Hoover, the President and Harry Daugherty had an hour in private after which the entire party proceeded to an outdoor stadium where sixty thousand people had gathered to hear Harding speak on Alaska.

Halfway through the speech, the President stumbled over his words. He dropped the manuscript and grasped the edge of the rostrum. The knuckles of his hands grew white. Sitting directly behind him, Hoover quickly picked up the fallen pages and put them in order. He saw the President's face: drawn, tense, lined with pain. Somehow, Harding managed to get through the speech, but as soon as he was finished, he hurried to his special train, canceling all engagements for that evening.

The next morning White House physician Dr. Charles Sawyer reported that Harding was suffering from some bad sea food and would require two days to recover.

The announcement may have quieted members of the press, but not Dr. Joel Boone, a young naval surgeon, who quickly sought out the Secretary of Commerce. "Mr. Hoover," he began, "I believe the President is suffering from something much worse than a digestive upset."

Alarmed, Hoover quickly called in other doctors. Their collective findings confirmed all suspicions. President Harding had suffered a serious heart attack.

The Secretary called Washington at once and advised the Secretary of State to keep in close touch with Calvin Coolidge, the Vice-President. However, by next afternoon, the President's condition had so much improved that Hoover called Secretary Hughes again and told him the worst seemed to be over.

It proved to be an idle hope. On the night of August 2, 1923, while Mrs. Harding was reading to her husband, Harding had another seizure. Doctors were quickly summoned but this time they could do nothing. In a few minutes Warren Gamaliel Harding, the twenty-ninth President of the United States, was dead, apparently of a heart attack.

EIGHT

Calvin Coolidge had hardly been sworn into office than the underlying scandals of the Harding adminstration broke out into the open.

The Teapot Dome affair hit the headlines first. Teapot Dome was a naval oil reserve in Wyoming originally set aside by the government to serve the nation's fuel needs in case of emergency. It had not been touched, even during the recent war. But sometime after Harding took office, his Secretary of the Interior, Albert Fall, had secretly leased the property to Harry Sinclair, the oil king. He had allowed a similar concession in Elks Hills, California, to Edward L. Doheny, another oil man. Subsequent investigations showed that Fall received $300,000 from the former deal and $100,000 from the latter. The leases were canceled at once and both Fall and Sinclair were tried and jailed, though for relatively short terms.

Following evidence of still more corruption, Herbert Hoover, who retained his post under Coolidge, urged him to remove Harry Daugherty as Attorney General, since few of these acts could have taken place without the knowledge, if not the connivance, of the man who headed the Justice Department.

However, the dour New Englander found it hard to

believe cabinet members capable of such corruption. After all, he had been in their midst for nearly an entire term as Vice-President and *he* hadn't seen anything out of line. But when Hoover, Hughes and Mellon persisted, Coolidge finally replaced Daugherty with Harlan F. Stone, who promptly brought the law down upon Harding's old cronies.

Convictions, though, were not easy to get. Twice Daugherty faced trial on charges of accepting kickbacks and handing out illegal prison pardons. Twice he escaped because of hung juries. Actor-cowboy Will Rogers, a pithy observer of the times, said that juries in these days seldom found a person guilty when they secretly admired him for having gotten away with it.

Such was the morality of the 1920s. Cynicism was the password. Excitement was king. Jazz, flaming youth and bootleg gin became the trademark of the times.

In the meantime, nothing very much changed except that a measure of honesty was restored in government. Business went on as usual. Industry was heavily subsidized, taxes were cut, and tariffs kept high. When Congress passed farm-support bills, Coolidge vetoed them. He hated to spend money and consistently opposed Hoover who asked for more funds to develop dams and waterways. It was a wonder such projects as the seven-state Colorado River plan, the Columbia River Basin and the San Joaquin Valley development program in California survived.

In spite of Coolidge's parsimony, Hoover assisted him in the 1924 presidential campaign by making several major speeches in his behalf. With the Democrats badly split that year, "Silent Cal" won hands down. The country then settled back for four more years of "Coolidge prosperity."

Meanwhile, the Hoovers enjoyed a period of relative calm. Herbert, Jr., graduated from Stanford in 1924 as an engineer and was married the year after; his brother Allan entered college that same year, also at Stanford. The family dream house near the campus was finally completed. Hoover now had time to classify the thousands of documents, films, maps and pamphlets relating to the late World War and its aftermath. These he donated to his alma mater, which eventually compiled them into the Hoover Library of War, Revolution and Peace, one of the great repositories of contemporary history.

As Secretary of Commerce, Hoover took part in a unique experiment on April 7, 1927, the first television broadcast in history. Standing before cameras in Washington, D.C., his image was seen by an audience in New York City. Those first telecasts were crude affairs; not until twenty years later did television become a technical, social and economic reality.

That same spring, Hoover assumed field leadership in relief work once again when the Mississippi River and its tributaries went on a rampage over a twelve-state area. For the next two months he directed units of the Army, Navy, Coast Guard and Public Health Agency as they fought one of the worst flood disasters in the nation's history. For him, housing the homeless and feeding the hungry were old stories. But for millions of Americans who saw him in the newsreels and heard him on the radio, Herbert Hoover was a legend come to life. The man who had helped rescue millions in Europe was no myth. Here he was, doing the same thing in his own country, on behalf of his fellow citizens!

Hoover looked back on his two-term service as Secretary of Commerce with immense satisfaction. Over the past seven years he had built a well-knit, purposeful organization in place of the sprawling series of unrelated bureaus he had inherited in 1921. He had recognized radio and aviation in their infancy and planned for their later growth. He had encouraged American business; set in motion huge water conservation projects; supported organized labor when labor had few friends. He had even favored unemployment insurance under private auspices as early as January 1923, only to be ignored by the insurance industry, which "did not even wish to experiment with it," as he sadly recalled.

He was ignored as well by President Coolidge when he warned against overspeculation and easy credit in the business world. "The outstanding instance," he said, "was the rising boom and orgy of mad speculation which began in 1927, in respect to which he [Coolidge] rejected or sidestepped all our anxious urgings and warnings to take action."

In spite of these misgivings, Hoover was able to write: "Any summation of Mr. Coolidge's services to the country must conclude that America is a better place for his having lived in it."

And what did the President think of his Secretary of Commerce? Apparently he was of two minds. Biographer David Hinshaw quoted Coolidge as saying, "If five Americans were to be selected on the basis of merit and ability to devise remedies for the present condition of the world—Herbert Hoover's name would head the list."

But historian Arthur Schlesinger, Jr., presented a startling contradiction. When Coolidge left the White House, he was quoted as having said about Hoover: "That man gave me unsolicited advice for six years, all of it bad!"

Obviously there was some lack of communication between the two men, not surprising, in view of Coolidge's tight-lipped approach to many problems. The nation, too, found "Silent Cal" something of a puzzle, especially after his coy announcement, "I do not choose to run for President in 1928."

Once Coolidge declared his ambiguous position, Hoover's name popped up everywhere. His long record in relief work both at home and abroad, and his quiet efficiency as Secretary of Commerce, had won him many supporters. But he would not make a move for the Presidency without consulting Coolidge.

He tried twice to draw out "Silent Cal." Neither time could he get a direct reply. Finally, when friends insisted on entering his name in the Ohio presidential primary, Hoover put it up to Coolidge bluntly. "Mr. President, twelve Ohio Congressmen, two former Governors, the state's leading newspaper and a deluge of individuals are urging me to enter the Ohio primary. I will not do so if you yourself want your name to be filed."

Coolidge remained silent.

"Let me put it another way, Mr. President. Will you *allow* your name to be entered in the Ohio primary?"

"No," was all he said.

"Well, then, may I file mine?"

"Why not?" came the reply.

"Therefore," Herbert Hoover jotted down in his memoirs, "I accepted the invitation of my Ohio friends on February 12, 1928."

He won the Ohio primary by a handsome margin and did even better in Massachusetts. As early as May, he was told that at least four hundred delegates would vote for him at the national convention. But Hoover still could not get Coolidge off his mind. Shouldn't he make one more effort to get the President to run?

He approached him again. "I am told there are four hundred delegates committed to me, Mr. President. I'm sure I can swing their votes over to you, provided you give the word."

"If you have that many," a skeptical Coolidge replied, "then you'd better keep them."

Hoover made no further overtures. Nor did he make any political speeches or issue any statements about his candidacy. "So far as I was concerned," he said, "the party should make its decision on the basis of my public record."

His friends now carried the preconvention campaign banner for him. They organized volunteer groups all over the country; some were political veterans, many were men and women with whom he had worked in the past. The Republican Old Guard, suspicious of their zeal, dubbed them Hoover's "Boy and Girl Scouts."

When the Republican National Convention met in Kansas City, Missouri, in June 1928, it was of practically one mind. A tremendous demonstration started as soon as Hoover's name was put in nomination. Listening to the proceedings over the radio in his Washington home, Hoover felt a glow of satisfaction as the voting got under way. The result of the first ballot, 837 out of a possible 1084 delegate votes, assured him of the nomination. The second ballot made it unanimous, in spite of some grumbling by the Old Guard.

Hoover's running mate was Charles Curtis, Senator from Kansas. A tall, dark-haired man with intense black eyes, he provided a strong contrast to Hoover, though the backgrounds of the two men had one strong similarity—hard work. Curtis, the great-great-grandson of an Osage Indian chief, had worked his way out of the prairies to law school and eventually to Congress.

Hoover's Democratic opponent in 1928 was the "Happy Warrior," cigar-smoking, derby-wearing, genial Alfred E. Smith, who had worked his way up from New York City politics to national party leadership. It would have been difficult to find two candidates more different in appearance than the rough, tough, smiling Irish Roman Catholic Smith and the precise, reserved, almost ponderous Quaker Hoover.

Issues divided them as well. Smith was an out-and-out

"wet" who favored repeal of the Volstead Act, which Congress had passed in 1919. As the Eighteenth Amendment to the Constitution, it prohibited the manufacture, distribution and sale of intoxicating liquors for beverage purposes.

Hoover, on the other hand, supported Prohibition. "Our country has deliberately undertaken a great social and economic experiment, noble in motive and far-reaching in purpose," he said. As turned around by his opponents, the phrases came out "noble experiment," a sarcastic reference to Hoover's puritanical attitude toward prohibition.

The two men disagreed on farm policies as well. Smith favored the McNary-Haugen Bill, which sought to put a price support under farm produce. Hoover opposed the bill, although he had advocated a similar practice for wholesalers as Food Administrator during and immediately after the World War.

Tariff was another issue which separated them. The Democrats, traditionally free-traders, promised to lower trade barriers if placed in office. Hoover ran on the Republican platform of high tariffs and protective policies for America's farms and factories.

Hoover also chose to make an issue of "collectivism." He charged that the McNary-Haugen Bill was supported by radical farmers. As he saw it, a growing left-wing movement, embracing many of the intelligentsia, was flocking to Governor Smith's support. He charged that a Smith victory would mean that the government would go into the power business. And since the "United States already was being infected from the revolutionary cauldrons of Europe," he was "determined that the Republican Party should draw the issue of the American system, as opposed to all forms of collectivism."

In other matters, there was no great difference between Governor Smith and Hoover. They agreed on reform of the judicial procedure; the prison system; the promotion of child welfare; better housing; the elimination of national wastes; better organization of the Federal Government; control of immigration; development of water resources; and oil conservation.

The 1928 campaign was clean on top, dirty beneath the surface. Vicious *sub rosa* attacks were made against Al Smith's religion. Hoover promptly denounced them, saying neither he nor his party wanted support on that basis.

Equally malicious charges were leveled against Hoover. Some said he was a British subject. His registration as an American citizen while living in Britain put an end to that rumor. Others accused him of robbing a Chinese family while in the Far East. An indignant letter from Tong Shao-yi, Hoover's old friend in China, and now Prime Minister of his country, publicly denied the charge.

To the credit of both candidates, neither condoned nor took part in such back-biting.

Hoover did not believe in easy campaigning. Since he had never used a ghost writer in the past, he refused to use one now. He worked over his paragraphs carefully, requiring two or three weeks to prepare each major speech. He made seven such addresses that fall. All were carried over radio, now an important communications device.

Among his campaign stops was a nostalgic return to West Branch, Iowa, after forty-two years.

His old home town hadn't changed much; there were more automobiles, of course, and fewer wagons, more gas stations than stables. The population was about the same, too; a thousand, give or take a few, just about what it had been when he was a boy.

There were still a few familiar faces left, now old and lined and nodding in memory of little Bertie. "Who'd ever believe he'd be runnin' for President now?" a toothless old farmer cackled.

"His dad, that's who!" another ancient retorted. "I well remember Jesse Hoover sayin' someday his boy would be in the White House, but we all just smiled and drank his cider."

"Well, he ain't there yet. Not that I don't think he'll make it, not for a minute!"

West Branch that day became a metropolis as fifteen thousand people from miles around came to see and hear the local boy who had made good. "The American people," he said to them and the nation, "have a fundamental conflict to resolve: American individualism versus the philosophy of government operation and control." The good folk of West Branch nodded in agreement.

So did an overwhelming majority of their fellow citizens on Election Day, 1928. They gave Hoover fifty-eight percent of the popular vote, a landslide. His electoral college vote margin was even wider: 444 to Smith's 87.

There were many reasons for Al Smith's defeat. "The issues which defeated the governor were general prosperity, Prohibition, the farm tariffs, Tammany, and the 'snuggling' up of the Socialists," the victorious candidate said.

Did Smith's religion contribute to his loss? Hoover didn't think so. "Had he been a Protestant, he would certainly have lost and might even have had a smaller vote. In fact," he went on somewhat smugly, "the religious issue had no weight on the final result."

Alfred Smith did not agree. "Neither the tariff nor the farm problem was important," he stated in his autobiography. "In its broad aspect the campaign appeared to me to be one of Smith or anti-Smith. A great many people predicate their vote on something that they are against rather than something they are for." And he made no bones about what he thought the majority of voters were against: his religion and his stand on Prohibition.

However Hoover and Smith differed over the issues or causes, they maintained a high personal respect for each other. Shortly after the 1928 elections, Al Smith noted: "I paid a friendly visit to Mr. Hoover and we told each other stories of the lighter side of campaigning for the presidency."

Following a long six-week good-will tour of Latin America, President-elect and Mrs. Herbert Hoover returned to the United States tanned, rested and eager to face the challenge that awaited them.

NINE

INCOMING PRESIDENT HERBERT HOOVER TOOK HIS oath of office on March 4, 1929, on a cold, wet, miserable day.

Americans couldn't care less about the weather. Most of them were basking in the glow of prosperity. Only the farmers were grumbling but few paid them much attention, to the nation's later regret. In the urban centers jobs were plentiful, wages high, money easy to borrow and anybody who "couldn't turn over a quick buck" had to be either lazy or asleep. The economy was moving and a man could bet on it.

Men did, mostly in the stock market. Large numbers of small investors had discovered Wall Street during the 1920's, until then the preserve of the Morgans, Rothschilds, DuPonts, Rockefellers and other giants of American finance. But now the little man was getting into the act and liking it. It was easy to take the plunge—just call a stockbroker. A hundred dollars in cash could buy him five hundred dollars' worth of stock, and if the price went up, he'd make a profit on the whole five hundred dollars!

"It's called buying on *margin*!" one novice investor explained to an admiring friend. "Twenty percent down is all you pay! The broker puts up the rest. The way things are, prices are bound to go up, so what can you lose?"

He didn't stop to explain what would happen if prices fell. In that event, the banker who had loaned money to the broker to finance margin purchases would call for additional cash to secure the loan. The broker, in turn, would demand more money from the investor. If the investor couldn't deliver, the broker had no choice but to sell his stock in order to raise cash. The stockholder, especially one with limited means, would then, in effect, be wiped out.

But few entertained such gloomy thoughts early in 1929. The market continued "bullish," the term used to describe an upward trend in prices, just as it had for the past three years. There was no reason in the world, absolutely none that investors could see, why they shouldn't go on "making a killing" month after month.

Just before the presidential torch passed from Republican Coolidge to Republican Hoover, the outgoing Chief Executive assured the country that its prosperity was absolutely sound and that stocks were cheap at current prices. Another wave of buying lifted prices to new highs.

The incoming President, however, was more cautious. "The stock market," Hoover said, "was blowing great guns when I came into the White House. Being fully alive to the danger, my first reaction was to get it under restraint."

He did this by requesting the Federal Reserve Board to raise the interest rate on loans and thus increase the cost of borrowing money. By so doing, he hoped to slow down the amount of speculation on margin. But the Board delayed action.

"The initial difficulty," Hoover explained, "was lack of government authority. To ask Congress for powers to interfere in the stock market was futile and, in any event, for the President to dictate the price of stocks was an expansion of presidential power without any constitutional basis."

This phrase—*without constitutional basis*—proved to be the key to his later difficulties in office. In an effort to live up to the Constitution as he saw it Hoover was often slow to upset tradition and depart from the past.

The Federal Reserve Board did, at last, boost interest rates that summer. "But people who dreamed of 100 percent profit in a week were not deterred by an interest rate of twenty percent a year," Hoover complained. "Control of interest rates could not stop them."

The boom went on. General Electric soared to 396, more than three times its price of a year ago. RCA gained sixty points in two weeks. U.S. Steel, American Can, A.T.&T. and other stocks reached new highs as the "little man" hugged himself for getting something for nothing.

Hoover had qualms about the boom, no doubt about that. He tried to get his feelings across to the American public by asking national editors to send out economic distress signals, which they dutifully did. But nobody was in the mood to listen, much less slow down. The speculation throttle was wide open, all the way.

This could well have been the result of Hoover's own optimism. At his inauguration only a few months ago, he had said: "I have no fears for the future of our country. It is bright with hope."

The fifty-five-year-old Chief Executive approached the Presidency as an engineer might, with blueprint in hand. "I came to the White House with a program in three directions," he explained.

First, he sought reforms in business and labor, and asked for more regulation of both for "the protection of liberty against misuse and abuse." Second, he wanted to overhaul governmental machinery, all but neglected since the Wilson administration. And third, he wanted to move America more rapidly into the realm of international cooperation and peace.

To help him construct this framework, he selected the ten ablest men he could find for his cabinet. For Secretary of State he chose Henry L. Stimson to succeed Frank B. Kellogg, a holdover from the previous administration who agreed to stay on until July 1929. His Attorney General was William D. Mitchell, while the Treasury post went to banker Andrew Mellon who had also served under Coolidge. Patrick J. Hurley became his Secretary of War after Hoover's original choice, James Good, died shortly after taking office; his Secretary of the Navy was Charles Francis Adams, descendant of the famous New England family. As Postmaster General, he selected

Walter F. Brown; Arthur Hyde was named to Secretary of Agriculture and his old Stanford classmate, Dr. Ray Lyman Wilbur, became Secretary of the Interior. Hoover's former post in Commerce went to Robert P. Lamont, while his Secretary of Labor was James J. Davis until 1930, after which William Doak took over.

The new President and his Cabinet never had a chance to get started. By the time a special session of Congress had muddled through an inconclusive tariff debate in November 1929, the nation was suffering the panic of the Great Depression.

When did the Depression actually begin?

And what were some of its main causes?

To answer the first question is to answer, in part, the second.

As good a starting point as any is October 24, 1929—"Black Thursday"—when the bottom fell out of the stock market for the first time. As in most points of origin, however, many factors leading to the Wall Street crash must first be taken into account. President Hoover cited several.

To begin with, he blamed the economic recessions in Europe for triggering the collapse in America. The currency difficulties on the continent, he said, were the result of the War of 1914–1918. Many economists were in substantial agreement.

Second, he pointed to the uncontrolled speculation of the late 1920s. He accused a number of American financiers of manipulating stocks and securities, regardless of their merits. "The financial world, instead of providing merely the lubricants of commerce and industry . . . often set itself up to milk the system," he charged. A strong accusation, but one which was shared by many responsible observers.

The President also put some of the blame on American banks, which he called the weakest link in our whole economic system. He singled out the inflationary policies of the Federal Reserve Board—the lowering of interest rates to member banks in 1927, for example—as one of the key factors in the crash. Again, no dissent. Loans for speculative purposes had zoomed to $8.5 billion by September 1929, up from $3.5 billion in 1927.

In contrast, there was a dramatic decline in building contracts; down to $216 *million* in 1929 from the 1927–1928 figure of $1.3 *billion* in 1927.

Equally disturbing was the drop in consumer spending. The United States rate slipped from 7.5 percent in 1927 to 1.5 percent in 1929. Why? For one thing, agriculture was far behind the booming industrial market; farmers had little cash and a lot of debts. The same was true of white-collar workers or anyone who lived on a limited fixed income. Thus, a substantial part of the American public remained out of the market place except for their most essential needs.

Meanwhile, the nation's production lines, thanks to more efficient methods, were turning out more and more goods for fewer and fewer buyers. As a result, merchandise piled up in the warehouses. The public sale of automobiles, radios, appliances, clothes, shoes, furniture and other major items slowed down. Even so, production and efficiency went on and on.

As Hoover described it: "By our own energies of invention and enterprise productivity per person increased thirty percent, a ratio without parallel. As a result of distortions in this advance, some adjustments were due."

Many historians have called this the understatement of the decade. The adjustments that followed were many, severe and painful.

The market, which had been showing steady increases in the spring of 1929, suddenly turned erratic during the summer months. Prices fell, then rose, then fell again. Nothing to worry about, experts said. They called it "corrective settling," a breather before the next upsurge.

A few wise investors read the signs and ducked out. In response, Charles E. Mitchell, chairman of the National City Bank of New York, assured the public not to be alarmed. "I know of nothing fundamentally wrong with the stock market or with the underlying business and credit structure," he said on Tuesday, October 22, in spite of the persistent rumbles on Wall Street.

This remark, together with some earlier easy lending practices by Mitchell, who also served as a director of the New York State Federal Reserve Bank, brought additional warnings from President Hoover, but little in the way of action, since he maintained it was up to Franklin Delano Roosevelt, then Governor of New York State, to control speculation on the New York Stock Exchange.

A new wave of selling hit the market on the twenty-third of October. The ticker ran 104 minutes late, a sure sign of trouble. Losses of fifty leading stocks averaged 18 points that day. Brokers looked at one another grimly as they closed their offices. Prices had dipped far too low to be called "corrective settling."

When the stock market opened on Thursday morning, the order of the day was: "Sell!" But who was there to buy? Where was all the money? Finding no support, prices skidded.

"Sell at any price!" frantic investors pleaded, unwilling or unable to meet mounting margin demands. Meanwhile, prices continued to drop, then fell again even before sell orders could be recorded, much less executed.

The panic—dreaded word on Wall Street—was on!

In Washington, Hoover followed the selling blizzard with mounting concern. "The ticker is an hour late," a Treasury aide telephoned from New York. "The big board is swamped! Sell orders are coming in from all parts of the country. There's a rumor, Mr. President, that a group of bankers are forming a buying trust to keep the market from falling out of sight!"

Shortly after noon the rumor was confirmed. Half a dozen New York bankers pooled nearly $250 million to buy stocks and thus brake the selling panic. Their action succeeded temporarily. For the rest of the day prices remained depressed but stable.

Hoover surveyed the wreckage. In an effort to maintain stability he told the nation: "The fundamental business of the country, that is, production and distribution of commodities, is on a sound and prosperous basis . . ."

The market, however, did not seem to be tuned in. When it opened on Monday, October 28, it took another fearful tumble, then followed with an even worse collapse the following day.

The shock waves from Wall Street reached the already shaky exchanges of London, Paris, Berlin and Rome. Linked to America and to each other through financial ties, they watched in despair as their own stocks gave way.

By mid-November 1929, Wall Street indices had sunk to their lowest point in years. In something like two weeks, American investors had lost more than $30 billion; stocks had dropped forty percent in values. One business magazine called the crash ". . . the financial catastrophe of the ages."

And catastrophe it was. Many businesses closed. Some banks failed. Factories shut down. Jobs became scarce. Suddenly it occurred to observers that things of this nature had been happening all summer long, especially in the industrial Northeast and on the farms, but that few had been paying attention to them. The crash merely intensified the collapse.

A deeply troubled Herbert Hoover knew something had to be done, but what? Never before had a President faced a crisis of such proportions. Moreover, no Chief Executive in the past had believed that this was any concern of the government's. It was a private matter, belonging strictly to the business community. As Hoover explained it: "Presidents steadfastly had maintained that the Federal Government was apart from such eruptions; they had always been left to blow themselves out." At least, that's what Van Buren, Grant, Cleveland and Theodore Roosevelt had done before him.

That was all Hoover had to go on. But the enormity of the present situation simply could not tolerate a passive attitude on his part. And he knew it. "The prime needs," he said, "were to prevent bank panics, and to mitigate the privation among the unemployed and the farmers." But because of little or no Federal experience in these matters, he had to make his way carefully, like a pioneer exploring uncharted territory.

With the support of a majority of his Cabinet, the President drew up a series of recommendations aimed at recovery. "The record will show," he wrote of those efforts, "that we went into action within ten days [of the crash] and were steadily organizing each week and month thereafter to meet the changing tides—mostly for the worse."

Why did these tides change "for the worse"?

And could Herbert Hoover have chosen a different course in those desperate days that might have made the Depression journey less painful for him and the nation?

He admitted many years later that "we could have done better."

One of the President's greatest consolations during these difficult days in office was the constant loyalty and devotion of his wife. A gracious First Lady, she brought charm and sensitivity to the White House.

Lou Hoover restored the historical mansion to its former quiet elegance after the somewhat bleak New England decor favored by the Coolidges. She moved in her own household goods collected over a lifetime of world travel. Together with period furniture she found in the White House attic, she gave the President's home "a more livable feeling," as her husband described it.

One of the Hoovers' first decisions was to re-convert a large upstairs bedroom to the original President's study, not used as such since McKinley's time. Here, in the spacious room where Abraham Lincoln signed the Emancipation Proclamation, Herbert Hoover struggled with his own affairs of state.

He also combined the new with the old. He was the first President to have a telephone on his desk, and had a special switchboard installed in order to keep in close touch with key members of his administration.

"We kept all the servants," Hoover recalled, including Catherine, the head cook, whom they found packing the day after the inauguration.

"But why are you leaving?" the First Lady wanted to know.

"Begging your pardon, mum, you'll not be needing me now. I voted for Al Smith, I did," she answered.

Lou Hoover suppressed a smile. She assured Catherine her political faith was her own affair. "We are far more interested in your cooking," she said.

"Which was superb," the President remembered.

Soon after, a medical crisis involving the older of the two Hoover sons became a family treat as things turned out. Herbert, Jr., now a father of two and working as an engineer in Boston, came down with tuberculosis and was immediately dispatched to a sanitarium. Whereupon his parents insisted his wife and two youngsters, Herbert III and Peggy-Ann, move in with them. The White House had plenty of rooms; 132 of them, as a matter of fact.

"Having Margaret [the President's daughter-in-law] and the children stay with us was a continuous joy," Grandfather Hoover recalled. Happily, after a year, Herbert, Jr., recovered and returned to Boston with his family. In time, a third grandchild was born to the Hoovers.

Another frequent visitor to the White House was Allan, the younger son, who graduated from Stanford in 1929. In the years following his marriage in 1937, Allan added three more grandchildren to the Hoover clan, including a delightful little beauty named Lou Henry.

During his term, the President sought relief from the rigors of office at a rustic mountain retreat in the Blue Hills of Virginia which he bought with his personal funds. Here, a hundred miles from Pennsylvania Avenue, he donned hip boots, stoked his pipe and waded into the Rapidan River, fly rod in hand. For a blissful few hours Hoover the President became Hoover the fisherman, his favorite role. Some years later, he presented the entire property to the Boy and Girl Scout organizations.

Both the President and the First Lady maintained a strong interest in young people throughout their careers. Mrs. Hoover, who had been national president of the Girl Scouts of America during her husband's service as Commerce Secretary, now became its honorary chairman. Hoover himself gave much of his time and effort to the cause of child welfare. In the summer of 1929 he called a national conference on the health and protection of children, one result of which was his famous "Children's Bill of Rights."

"For every child," it began, "spiritual and moral training to help him stand firm under the pressure of life."

There were eighteen other pronouncements, each one dealing with a child's basic needs: a secure home life, good health, adequate diet, education, recreation, guidance and protection from exploitation. The document ended with a stirring resolve: "For every child these rights, regardless of race, or color, or situation, wherever he may live under the protection of the American flag."

Herbert Hoover's warm concern for children never lagged. Some of his answers to letters addressed to him, later published as a book, were charming and delightful.

"What do you think is essential for success?" a schoolboy asked him. Hoover's reply carried three essentials: "First, religious faith and morals; second, education including college; and third, do not neglect being just a boy. It only comes once."

A few were tinged with controversy. For example, he expressed himself strongly against socialized medicine; his privilege certainly. But he also came up with a curious reply to a seventh grader who asked him what he thought of social studies. "I do not believe in it at all," Hoover wrote back. "Social studies should be deferred for a long time—preferably when you get to college."

This bluntness—some have called it refusal to adapt to ways and ideas other than his own—was strikingly evident during his Presidency. For example, he refused to engage in "log-rolling," the subtle art of political give and take. For him only the facts were enough. A man's decisions, he felt, must be made on the merits of a case. All else was so much dross.

Another handicap was his extreme sensitivity, hidden behind that stolid appearance and stiff high collar. He tended to regard opposition to his program as personal attacks on his values. He failed to see that political philosophies of others could legitimately differ from his own.

It was the opinion of many close friends and associates that Hoover suffered as a public figure because he could not reach out and touch people emotionally. He gave the impression of being aloof, and perhaps he was. As one of his friends has pointed out, Hoover distrusted the masses and scorned the idle rich.

Lack of personal "color" also hurt Hoover, especially in a time of storm and stress, when the nation was looking for a symbol of leadership. But with his basic integrity, he refused utterly to become a political acrobat. He tore up press releases in which he was cast in a heroic mold. His speeches, for example, were honest, serious, well-organized—and drab.

Thus, his inability or unwillingness to communicate on the level of the common man, to adjust to issues, to give ground to his opponents, led him into conflicts all during his Presidency. Nowhere was this more apparent than in the field of unemployment relief, perhaps the biggest single problem of his administration.

TEN

"I WILL USE EVERY DOLLAR OF CASH THE GOVERNment has and every dollar it can borrow to help take care of every individual in need, but that is not the way to do it."

This was the substance of the remark made by Herbert Hoover to a close friend shortly after the start of the Depression. The President's conviction that government spending "was not the way to do it" has sometimes been called his political philosophy in a nutshell. Not that he was unwilling to dip into the Federal Treasury to provide relief. He eventually did to a greater extent than any President up to his time. But he stubbornly refused to take that step until all voluntary and local resources had been exhausted. And sometimes not even then, to the anger and frustration of many of his fellow citizens.

Hoover brought to the Presidency a strong aversion to Federal action in areas he felt belonged to the private sector, in particular, the problem of unemployment relief. After all, voluntary efforts had fed and housed the needy of Europe after the war and in the great Mississippi floods of 1927. Governments had helped, yes; they had contributed money, equipment and men. But the organization and execution, and much of the funds, had been supplied by private groups and individuals. A nationwide economic collapse, therefore, seemed not very different in size, scope and need from widespread famine or flood. A catastrophe like the others. Hoover firmly believed it could best be met by private, voluntary action.

His formula was simplicity itself: neighbor helping neighbor, employer helping employee, the rich giving to the poor, and everyone in need helping himself to the hilt.

In his initial relief message to the nation, Hoover said: "The best hearts and brains of every community could best serve their neighbors." Local responsibility, he solemnly declared, "was the basis of American life." He pointed out that "centralized bureaucracy gives the sufferers more red tape than relief," and warned that politics in such matters "must be shunned as a plague."

He worked day and night to put these high-minded ideals into practice. He obtained pledges from businessmen to keep factories working. He asked labor not to strike except as a last resort and warned employers against lockouts. He encouraged locally sponsored public works and siphoned off a limited amount of Federal money into dams, bridges and roads. He asked employers to look after the private relief of their own labor force, and to share the work load among as many workers as possible. He favored easy credit for business expansion and utilized the buying power of Federal agencies to prop up agricultural prices. And he pushed for the passage of a flexible tariff act to protect American farmers and labor against competition from abroad.

The Hoover effort gave the nation a hopeful outlook. Employment picked up in some areas. Stock prices began to climb back to their pre-1929 levels. Thus encouraged, he announced early in 1930 that "all the evidences indicate that the worst effects of the crash upon unemployment will have passed during the next sixty days."

As it turned out, President Hoover's predictions were hasty. Despite his efforts to establish a sound economy, the leaders of business found it impossible to follow his advice and unemployment was increasing. Private spending was simply not maintaining 1929 levels.

Hoover's critics maintained that if he had depended more on Federal funds in the winter of 1929–1930 and less on promises of private spending, the breakdown that followed the initial spurt might have been checked.

The split between Hoover and his critics widened in the summer of 1930 as the business crises deepened. Many economists on both sides of the political fence put much of the blame for this on the passage of the Smoot-Hawley Tariff Act.

This restrictive trade bill had been fifteen months in the making. It was the work of two fervent protectionists, one of whom, Senator Reed Smoot of Utah, had voted against America's entry into the League of Nations. The bill's admitted aim was to keep the United States "self-contained and self-sustaining," in Congressman Hawley's own words. Enactment of such a law had been a key plank in the 1928 Republican platform, and now President Hoover considered it a matter of honor to push for it.

It was also, in his opinion, a matter of economic necessity. He warned the American farmer that if foreign butter, pork, beef, beans, wheat and wool were brought into the United States without a sufficiently high tariff, "your produce would rot on your farms."

He was bitterly attacked for this stand, in and out of Congress. Bankers, economists, editors and businessmen from both sides of the political fence urged him to veto the bill. Instead, Hoover signed it into law on June 17, 1930, even though he admitted it had flaws which, he hoped, could be adjusted later on.

Who was for the bill? Not surprisingly, such high-tariff advocates as the National Grange, the Farmers Union, the American Farm Bureau Federation and the American Federation of Labor.

In the opinion of many of Hoover's contemporaries, then and since, the Smoot-Hawley Tariff Act brought economic disaster to the United States and to the world trading community at large. By putting a high tax on imports, it discouraged foreign goods from entering the United States, one of the great buying markets of the world. In retaliation, foreign nations raised *their* tariffs against American goods, and effectively blocked U.S. exports. Thus international trade, constantly beset by troubles ever since the Great War, became bogged down even more.

All through his term and long after, Herbert Hoover insisted that the Smoot-Hawley Act had little to do with the business slump at home and abroad. He winced at the charge that it extended the Depression; he pointed out that the bill became law *after* the Wall Street crash. Few questioned his facts on timing. It was his reasoning that came under attack.

Hoover presented evidence that only a small portion of incoming foreign goods was affected. True, his opponents answered, but these were highly strategic items, heavily rated in the economy of trading nations.

The President also cited percentages, saying, correctly, that the proportion of duty-free lists actually increased with the new bill. Percentages, his critics replied, had no relation to tonnage and value.

Hoover refused to concede defeat. He said the bill was really a progressive move, that Senator Joseph Grundy, an extreme protectionist, had attacked it as too liberal. And he stoutly denied that the Smoot-Hawley Act was, as his critics charged, the beginning of a world movement to increase tariffs.

His opponents jumped him on that last point. Hoover retorted that the attacks were politically inspired, as indeed many were. But the President also came under fire from observers *outside the realm of politics,* during and after his term of office.

The Encyclopaedia Britannica, which never ran for political office, bluntly refuted Hoover's assertion. "The upward revision of import duties of the United States was the first important step in this direction and was quickly followed by import restrictions on the part of other countries."

From this side of the ocean, the Encyclopedia Americana offered a similar appraisal. "The Hawley-Smoot Act was seized upon by manufacturing interests to obtain special favors for themselves. It raised the general level of rates about 20 per cent . . . and foreign countries retaliated by raising their own import duties."

Plummeting farm prices supplied the sorry evidence: wheat dropped from $1.05 a bushel in 1929 to 68 cents in 1930 to 39 cents in 1932; cotton fell from 16.8 cents a pound in 1929 to 9.5 cents, then to 6.5 cents. Other farm prices followed suit.

What could the poor farmer do now? The tractor he had bought on credit when wheat sold at a dollar a bushel had to be paid off three years later with wheat at 40 cents a bushel. It meant he had to grow two or three times as much wheat in order to pay off that tractor.

That in itself was bad enough. But the real tragedy hit him when he couldn't even sell that wheat, much less grow it!

Hoover himself brought the curtain down with the admission that during the 1932 campaign "raising the tariff from its sleep was a political liability despite the virtues of its reform."

The embattled President had his opponents in Congress as well. They gave him no peace; they hounded his every attempt at recovery. Among the most troublesome was Senator George W. Norris, an Independent-Republican who sharply disagreed with him over the operation of utilities. Norris favored Federal control on water and electric power. Hoover leaned to state and local operation.

Two other outspoken foes were Senators Edward P. Costigan of Colorado and Robert M. La Follette, Jr., of Wisconsin, who fought him on labor legislation and relief procedures. Another was Senator Robert Wagner of New York, whose son was to serve as Mayor of New York City for a dozen years. The senior Wagner was a constant thorn in Hoover's side in matters affecting labor and social legislation. So was Fiorello La Guardia, the firebrand Congressman from New York, who battled him on taxes, labor and general principles.

There were more: Senator Hugo Black of Alabama, Congressman John Nance Garner, the Democrat from Texas who became Speaker of the House under his administration and later Vice-President under another; Senator William G. McAdoo of California, Wilson's son-in-law, Senator William E. Borah of Idaho, and a number of others.

Hoover met their challenges head on. As in-fighting increased, as pressure mounted, he resorted to some politically unfortunate judgments. Norris, for example, he called "a devoted socialist." He accused La Guardia of demagoguery. Those who opposed his bills became "radicals." And he ignored La Follette, Jr., and Costigan, for reasons which became embarrassingly clear later in his administration.

But he was not a President alone. Hoover had friends in the White House and throughout the nation. Without exception, he had, at that time, the loyalty of every member of his Cabinet and the close friendship of a least one of them, Dr. Roy Lyman Wilbur, his former Stanford classmate. Bernard Snell, the Republican House leader, was another who was close to him, socially and politically. Senator Dwight Morrow he described as a tower of strength, in and out of Congress. Hoover also had a host of friends in the lesser echelons of government, many of whom had served under him in Belgian relief and in the Commerce Department. In addition, he had the friendship of many men in the worlds of business, education and finance. He was far from lonely in his Presidency, even when it seemed that most of Congress, the press and the voters were against him.

The tougher the going, the more determined Hoover became.

Habitually an early riser, the Chief Executive invited his staff to join him in a game of medicine ball on the White House lawn long before most people were stirring. The more active members of his Cabinet obliged, thus giving them the droll title "the medicine ball Cabinet."

After breakfast, which he shared sometimes with his family and sometimes with his advisors, Hoover was at his desk at eight-thirty each morning, six days a week. There, until ten o'clock at night, often later, he waded through the thousand and one details of the Presidency.

But for all his conscientious toil, there seemed no end of trouble in that troubled summer of 1930. The business slump in the middle of that year was followed by a widespread drought, the most severe in recent memory. Farmers all along the lower Mississippi, the Ohio valley and the Dakotas watched helplessly as crops shriveled and died for lack of moisture. More than a million families felt the effects of this cruel blow from nature. Twenty million head of cattle were lost or destroyed.

One vignette told the entire story. A weary farmer in Oklahoma squinted up at the blazing August sun. "Do yer darnedest, hear? Jes' burnin' up what don't sell in the market, anyways. You burn it or I will, what's the difference?" Then he turned away, too angry and too dry to spit at the parched, cracked soil.

The drought emergency presented the sort of problem Hoover could see and understand, one that did not defy solution, like many of his other difficulties in office.

Was it a question of property loss? He instructed his Secretary of Agriculture to bring in all pertinent facts on the extent and severity of drought damage.

Was it a question of relief administration? He called in the governors of the stricken areas and Red Cross officials. They came with recommendatons and set up committees to deal with problems on the spot.

Was it a question of money? President Hoover personally headed a Red Cross drive which pledged $10 million for drought relief. In his annual message to Congress that year he asked for a Federal appropriation of $30 million for seed and feed loans. He directed the Federal Land Bank and the Farm Board, both products of his administration, to expand credit facilities. He persuaded banks and insurance companies to hold off temporarily on mortgage collections.

Was it a question of supply distribution? Hoover called in the heads of the nation's railroads and promptly won their agreement to haul feed and relief supplies to drought areas at a fifty-percent reduction in rates.

And what about jobs for farmers unable to work because of crop failure? He directed that Federal highway funds be shifted to drought areas so more jobs would be available in those places. He did the same with governmental waterways and flood control projects.

Then Hoover sat back and surveyed the scene. By Thanksgiving of 1930, drought relief committees reported that acute distress had been averted, at least for the time being.

Agreement came from the Chicago Board of Trade, up to now not a very sympathetic friend of the President. "The prompt action from Washington," its directors said in a resolution, "alone prevented widespread panic in America."

But with one fire squelched, another soon flared up.

The Congressional elections in November 1930 returned a Democratic House of Representatives to Capitol Hill, a not unusual result in off-year balloting. The Republicans did manage to hold the Senate by the narrow margin of one vote, but growing hostility from rebellious party members all but placed the Upper House in the opposition camp as well. This split between the Executive and Legislative branches plagued the President all through his administration and, to some extent, justified his later complaints of Congressional delay and harassment.

Herbert Hoover had his hands full with still another problem: Prohibition, a product of the Volstead Act. He had inherited this clumsy bit of legislation from the Harding administration. With its spreading decay of crime, bootlegging and violence, prohibition clearly was not of his doing, though he himself was a "dry." "I should have been glad to have humanity forget all about strong alcoholic drinks," he wished heartily. "They are moral, physical and economic curses to the race."

He also knew it was impossible to enforce a measure which failed to get the full cooperation of local and state agencies. "In the present stage of human progress," he philosophized, "this vehicle of joy [alcohol] could not be generally suppressed by Federal law." But since it was the law of the land, he was honor bound, as its Chief Executive officer, to uphold it.

Being of two minds about the matter, Hoover appointed the Wickersham Commission in 1929 to look into the entire matter of Prohibition and its relation to crime. After more than a year of investigation, the commission came up with an equally divided report: it indirectly condemned the Volstead Act but recommended that it be kept on the books. Meanwhile, a cynical public hooted and howled and kept on supporting bootleggers and speakeasies while gangsters played a merry tattoo against each other with their sub-machine guns and sawed-off shotguns.

In spite of mounting evidence to the contrary, the President was certain most Americans were against repeal of the Eighteenth Amendment. "Up until the winter of 1932," he confessed, "I was convinced that major public opinion was in favor of retaining the Amendment."

It was to prove a case of recognition too late and too little action.

ELEVEN

IN 1887, WHEN HERBERT HOOVER WAS THIRTEEN years old, President Grover Cleveland, a Democrat, said that "though the people support the government, the government should not support the people."

In 1931, when Herbert Hoover was nearly fifty-seven years old, he modified Cleveland's philosophy somewhat by saying that if government support of the people was the only alternative to starvation, then "Federal aid we must have." But, he affirmed, "I have faith in the American people that such a day shall not come."

Such a day had come, in the opinion of many observers. But Hoover remained adamant almost to the end of his term. In his view, direct government aid to the unemployed was not necessary. This conviction earned him the bitter resentment of millions of Depression-mired souls, and his name, sometimes unjustly, became synonymous with public suffering.

Part of this unfortunate identification may have been due to misunderstandings on both sides, his and the public's; part to tactless statements made by himself and his staff. Part could be traced to Hoover's inherent belief that every individual should pull himself up by his own bootstraps, just as he himself had done. But most of all, it may have been because Hoover was so adamant about his economic views. His strong convictions on the subject of what government had no right to do greatly narrowed the field of his possible activities.

In the first year after the crash, the number of jobless rose to six million, about nine percent of the labor force as against the normal four or five percent during so-called "full employment" years. The out-of-work figure climbed to nine million in 1931, then to 13 million in 1932.

Few, before 1930, could have guessed the severity of the problem. Many conservatives and liberals alike were of the opinion that the Wall Street crash actually might have been a good thing. Its effects would pass. The unemployed would go back to work again, sooner or later, probably by the spring of 1930, they said.

The unemployed didn't, in spite of optimistic statements by government officials and business leaders. Hoover joined in this chorus. Yet he must have sensed harder times ahead. "Fearful of the inevitable increase of unemployment and distress in the winter of 1930–1931," he recalled, "I initiated the President's Committee for Unemployment Relief."

This was a voluntary effort in keeping with the Hoover credo. He named Colonel Arthur Woods, the energetic former Police Commissioner of New York, as chairman. With the cooperation of the states, the Woods Committee organized some three thousand local, nonpartisan groups throughout the nation to look after the care, feeding and housing of their less fortunate neighbors. In

Hoover's words, "They were given the primary responsibility to see that no one went hungry or cold."

A number of highly placed individuals strongly disagreed with the President's methods, among them Senator Borah of Idaho, a Republican. He demanded direct Federal payments—the British called them "doles"—to those in distress.

Hoover resisted. He said it would lead to waste and corruption, that it would influence voters. However, he had no objection to indirect Federal aid, which he defined as government funds for the construction of roads, dams, bridges and other public works, provided, as always, that their costs remained within the budget.

The fight between those for and those against Federal aid intensified. Name-calling began. Hoover referred to Borah and the groups he represented as "left-wingers." Borah retaliated by calling Hoover "heartless."

The President was deeply wounded and took his case to the public. "This is not an issue as to whether people shall go hungry and cold in the United States," he protested. "It is a question of the best method by which hunger and cold shall be prevented." To fall back on the dole, he said, would impair something infinitely valuable in the life of the American people, and would strike at the roots of self-government. "Self-help," he pleaded, "has been the American way of relieving distress, and the country is successfully meeting its problem in the American way today."

Then he concluded: "I do not feel that I should be

charged with lack of human sympathy for those who suffer."

Not lack of sympathy, his critics answered, but perhaps lack of insight and observation.

"The horrors of those terrible times . . . were terribly real to those who lived through them," John D. Hicks remembered. As a young history teacher during Hoover's years in the White House, he saw an America that seemed strikingly different from the one seen by some government officials and business leaders.

The Depression, in Hicks' eyes, was a time when "Savings disappeared . . . citizens . . . lost their homes . . . stores closed for lack of customers . . . theaters went dark; university enrollments dropped abysmally and faculty members lost their jobs or had their salaries cut . . . soup kitchens opened; bread lines began to form; local relief systems broke down; panhandlers roamed the streets; philanthropy dried up to a trickle; the jobless slept on park benches . . . and uncounted numbers knew the meaning of hunger and cold and fear."

Hoover, reviewing his first two years in office, was able to say that "despite and contrary to all the smearing, we got through the first phase of the Depression until the spring of 1931 and no one went hungry or cold—if our committees knew about it."

That, perhaps, was the heart of the trouble. The President's Committee did not, or could not, grasp the total picture of misery throughout the United States. The components were there, out in the open, for all to see.

The newspapers published photographs of a thousand jobless men waiting in line in New York City for a few low-paying jobs.

The newsreels ran motion pictures showing colonies of shacks built of tarpaper and packing crates and odd pieces of tin and lumber. Called "Hoovervilles," they sprung up in parks and empty lots, wherever one didn't have to pay rent.

Social workers in Chicago reported in the second winter of the Depression that men, women and children could be seen in the city dumps digging into heaps of refuse as soon as garbage trucks pulled out.

No one was more familiar with conditions such as these than Herbert Hoover. He had seen as much hunger and poverty as any other man of his generation. But he insisted his methods would see the country through. To fall back on huge government outlays to create jobs and hand out doles to the unemployed represented "a spirit of spending in the country which must be abandoned," he told Congress in January 1932. "Rigid economy is the real road to relief to every element of our population. We cannot squander our way to prosperity."

To which John Maynard Keynes, Hoover's champion at the 1919 Paris Peace Conference, replied, in effect, "Rubbish!" He told America: "This is not a crisis of poverty. This is a crisis of abundance." He urged the United States to abandon the gold standard, to spend, to go into debt if necessary in order to boost national income and to encourage consumption.

Another of Hoover's old friends also disagreed with

him. William T. Foster, who had saluted Hoover's business leadership in 1929, now challenged him with the remark, "We shall not restore good times, no matter what else we do, until we spend more."

But Hoover would not budge. "Nothing is more necessary at this time than to balance the budget," he insisted in 1932. To that end, he also proposed a rise in taxes, since incoming tax collections had fallen along with the economy.

And so the impasse continued.

Earlier, a crisis of another sort faced the President. In the spring of 1931, Arthur Woods, his chairman of the Committee for Unemployed Relief, submitted a request for an expanded public works program calling for slum clearance, low-cost housing and rural electrification. He also favored a bill by Senator Wagner that would provide for a national employment service under Federal direction. But Hoover rejected his recommendations, certain that his own program of self-help and local rule would do the job.

Whereupon Woods resigned "for reasons of health" and Hoover replaced him in August 1931 with Walter S. Gifford, president of the American Telephone and Telegraph Company. Five months later, a Senate Committee which included Robert La Follette, Jr., and Edward Costigan, both Democrats, questioned Gifford about the work of his relief organization.

An astonishing interview now took place. It appeared in none of the standard biographies on Hoover or, for that matter, in his own memoirs. But it was recorded in the minutes of the Senate Manufactures Committee, which met in January 1932, during the first session of the Seventy-second Congress.

Costigan and La Follette began by asking Gifford if he knew how many people were idle. Gifford replied that he did not. Then they asked him if he knew how many people were being aided by the committee's system of self-help. Gifford answered that he didn't know that, either.

Upon further questioning, Gifford revealed that he was not familiar with standards of assistance in the different states, nor could he tell the committee how much money had been raised by his volunteers.

How about local communities? the Senators prodded. Could Mr. Gifford estimate how much relief money they might be able to raise through taxation and borrowing? Mr. Gifford said he could not.

The president of the American Telephone and Telegraph Company, however, was not at a loss for opinions as far as the proposed Federal dole was concerned. He was against it. It would cut into private charity, he contended. It would be a disservice to those out of work. "The net result," he concluded, "might well be that the unemployed who are in need would be worse instead of better off."

His words were the echo of a remark made the year before by President Hoover. In opposing the idea of direct relief to the unemployed, Hoover had said that "the opening of the doors of the Federal Treasury is likely to stifle this [private] giving and thus destroy far more resources than the proposed charity from the Federal Government."

Still, Hoover never shut the doors on direct aid. "I am willing to pledge myself," he insisted, "that if the time should ever come that the voluntary agencies of the country together with the local and state governments are unable to find resources with which to prevent hunger and suffering in my country, I will ask the aid of every resource of the Federal Government."

But he never opened the doors very wide, either. For had he not pledged his administration to sound currency, economy and a balanced budget?

TWELVE

If Herbert Hoover's only major problem during his Presidency had been unemployment relief, his course might have been clearer, his moves more effective. But from the day he took office he faced a myriad of problems, many of them in the international field. "My ambition in our foreign policies," he said, "was to lead the United States in full cooperation with world moral forces to preserve peace."

It was not an ambition easily fulfilled. America was still isolationist. It still shunned the World Court and the League of Nations. "Our proper responsibilities," Hoover sadly admitted, "were thus neglected."

However, a ray of hope sustained him. The Kellogg-Briand Peace Pact, drawn up during Coolidge's administration, and signed in the summer of 1929, committed the United States and fourteen other nations to forgo force in the settlement of international disputes. But it lacked the teeth of collective military action, relying only on moral obligations. In the end, it turned out to be a scrap of paper, to blow away with the first strong wind of aggression.

Spurred on by the pact's apparent success, Hoover next called for a major disarmament conference with the hope of cutting down on military spending. By patient diplomacy, he convinced England to convene the London Naval Disarmament Conference early in 1930 in which the United States, Britain, France, Italy and Japan took part. After months of deliberation, three of the five nations—France and Italy had some reservations—agreed on a formula to limit the future construction of warships and aircraft carriers.

The Senate ratified the treaty in July 1930. Justifiably proud, Hoover announced that "by this act we have dismissed from the mind of the world any notion that the United States entertains ideas of aggression, imperial power or exploitation of foreign nations."

As much could not be said for Germany and Japan. Both were showing increasing signs of belligerent nationalism, frequently the prelude to military action.

Hoover was particularly disturbed about the situation in Germany. Burdened by heavy reparations under the Treaty of Versailles, Germany's economy alternated between wild inflation and political unrest. A shrill little man named Adolf Hitler, wearing a swastika on his arm and sporting a nervous mustache, was already raising a clamor against the Jews and Communists, whom he blamed for the real cause of the Reich's difficulties.

For some time now, Hoover had been thinking about a moratorium, a plan to defer payment of war debts. Such a move, he thought, might give Germany and Austria some much-needed breathing space to help shore up their economies. He therefore asked Congress to approve a one-year moratorium on reparations, provided all affected nations went along. Congress gave its approval. In time, fifteen nations agreed to postpone all war payments and acceptances for one year beginning in July 1931.

Stock markets picked up at once at home and abroad. Finance ministers talked of converting reparation money into capital expansion. Lines of credit began to stir. "I breathed easier," Hoover said of this turn of events. "There was a momentary lift in the economic world, but it lasted less than a week."

Reason for the relapse was clear. France, who had been receiving large reparations from Germany, had been painfully slow about signing the moratorium agreement. A six-week delay between Hoover's proposal and France's acceptance was just long enough for the fires of financial panic to jump the continent and reach the proud Bank of England. This prompted France to withdraw large amounts of her gold deposited in London. England, traditionally a free-trade nation, retaliated by slapping duties on incoming foreign goods for the first time in nearly a century.

This had a disastrous effect on America's economy. With trade barriers erected in England, the price of U.S. wheat, corn and cotton, already depressed for lack of world markets, took another tumble. The depression at home worsened under the impact of the British version of the Smoot-Hawley Tariff Act.

England took still another step: in a desperate move to retain her dwindling credits, she went off the gold standard. The rest of Europe recoiled immediately.

Commodity and security markets shut down all over the continent, thus blocking off further gold shipments to London.

The eyes of the world now turned to America. According to Hoover, Europe was of the opinion that the United States would be the next bulwark of international stability to collapse. He spent many anxious moments with Treasury officials and bankers to make certain that America would hold fast to the gold standard, no matter what.

For a while it was touch and go. Foreign nations, quite legally, began to raid United States gold reserves. "By the end of October [1931]," Hoover recalled, "we were to lose about $700,000,000 from our gold supply."

These withdrawals from abroad, Hoover wrote, "cramped our volume of credit. To add to our troubles, domestic hoarding of gold and currency began. Our exports to the world dropped to about one-third of the 1929 rate. Worse still, our exports of principal farm products to Europe dropped to about zero, further demoralizing commodity prices. Our unemployment swelled."

A better, and more bitter, record of the times would be hard to find.

In the midst of what Hoover called "this nightmare" came a chilling threat from the American Legion's annual convention in Detroit: a demand that the government pay the $3.4-billion veteran bonus now, and not in 1945, as Congress had agreed to do when it issued bonus certificates in 1925.

Hoover knew that such a move would seriously deplete the Treasury. He promptly boarded a plane to Detroit and made a personal plea to the Legion not to press for the bonus. "As a result," the President said with a sigh, "I staved off that blow for a while."

He then flew back to Washington for a series of grim sessions with bankers and insurance leaders. During the next two weeks, Hoover tried desperately to set up two associations. The first would extend liberal credits to businesses and banks in order to keep more of them from going under. The second would take the pressure off mortgage loans and thus cut the mounting rate of foreclosures on farms and homes. The financiers agreed, provided the government supplied the money. They would not involve their own funds for such questionable tactics.

But Hoover refused to put up Federal money, repeating his now familiar refrain: "Such a course [of government action] should be avoided if private enterprise were to perform its own functions."

On October 5, he was to feel more depressed than ever, and before some thirty-two thousand howling fellow citizens. The setting was the third game of the 1931 World Series played in Philadelphia between the Philadelphia Athletics and the St. Louis Cardinals. The President, an avid baseball fan from his youth, hoped his presence at a sporting event might be a gesture of reassurance to a country suffering from a severe attack of the "jitters."

In the midst of the game, an aide handed the President a telegram. Hoover read it; his face, already pale and drawn, became ashen. Stuffing the telegram into his pocket, he arose and slowly made his way up the aisle which was quickly cleared by security men. The presidential party followed close behind.

The sudden exit caught the attention of the crowd. A murmur of bewilderment swept through the stands. The outcome of the game was still in doubt—why was the President leaving? A few insolent fans, hiding behind the anonymity of the crowd, began to boo. Others joined in. Somebody called out "Beer!"

"Beer! Beer!" the crowd picked up the chant. "We want beer!" Prohibition was then still in effect.

They did not, could not, know the personal burden that had just been added to Hoover's already heavy load. The telegram, now stuck out of sight, had informed him that his close friend and associate, Senator Dwight Morrow, had just died.

The President's struggle to contain America's skidding economy went on. Despite a recalcitrant Democratic House, he strengthened the Federal Farm Board with government funds, for he was now beginning to accept the fact that private enterprise couldn't, or wouldn't, come to the aid of the farmer. He did the same for the hard-pressed homeowner with a system of Home Loan Banks. And he finally organized the National Credit Association, supported entirely by privately pooled funds, which would presumably bail out banks and business in trouble.

So many hopes, so few fulfilled! A month later, Hoover buried the Credit Association, one of his most cherished programs, with these words: "After a few weeks of enterprising courage the bankers' National Credit Association became ultraconservative, then fearful, and finally died. Its members, and the business world, threw up their hands and asked for government action."

As 1931 limped to a close, the economic handwriting on the wall became bold and clear. In order that the country should be absolutely assured that the government was in a position to meet any public necessity, the President came up with a bold new plan. "I proposed the establishment of a Reconstruction Finance Corporation, with a capital of $500,000,000 and authority to borrow up to $3,000,000,000 from either the Treasury or private sources." The time had come for Federal action and the President knew it.

The Reconstruction Finance Corporation was a brave step for an administration that had, for the most part, hidden behind the skirts of private enterprise. As Hoover visualized it, the RFC would make farm and crop loans to farmers, lend money to banks and insurance companies so they could postpone foreclosures, make loans to railroads, finance exports to help farmers and the unemployed (and undo the mischief of the Smoot-Hawley tariff!) and finance the construction of industrial plants. It also aimed at reform of bankruptcy laws, stock market practices, and the banking system itself. In scope and intent it was a Federally supported effort the likes of which the United States had never seen before. Obviously, Hoover had come to the point of no return.

But even here, he had a fight on his hands. Congressional Democrats now sensed that the Republicans were running scared, or at least were desperate enough to abandon their old positions. Why help them? Let the nation stew in the Republican juice for a while, then maybe, when national elections rolled around next fall, voters would think twice before returning them to power. And so the House, led by the bulldog tactics of John Nance Garner, fought the President every inch of the way over the RFC measure. After a six-week delay, the bill passed Congress and Hoover signed it into law in January 1932.

The President, though, wasn't out of the woods yet. Democrats charged that RFC loans went primarily to a few big banks and insurance companies, in spite of Hoover's denials to the contrary. Figures supplied by the President revealed that the new agency in its first three months of operation had loaned $126 million to banks in forty-five states. However, these figures took on a less virtuous aspect when it was discovered that over half this sum had gone to three large banks.

Nevertheless, in its first year of operation, the Reconstruction Finance Corporation pumped $1.5 billion in the national economy. Despite early controversy, it remained one of Hoover's finest efforts to keep a dangerously sick economy from expiring altogether.

As President, Herbert Hoover often had to deal with many problems at the same time. For example, while in the midst of organizing the RFC, the international pot began boiling again. This time it was in the Far East, where Japan, on the flimsiest of pretenses, launched an invasion of Manchuria.

Hoover strongly condemned the move as an "offense against the comity of nations" and an "affront to the United States." But when Secretary of State Stimson suggested a boycott against Japanese goods in order to put some starch into America's protests, Hoover demurred. "Sanctions," he told his Cabinet, "could lead to war."

America's indignation, so long as it remained verbal, made little difference to Japan. She continued her invasion of Manchuria, then attacked Shanghai, far to the south. Eventually the case went before the League of Nations, which found Japan guilty of aggression. But the Emperor shrugged his shoulders and instructed his foreign minister to walk out of the League. It was as simple as that for a strong nation in those days to take the law into her own hands, providing the rest of the world stood by.

In the meantime, war of another sort was building up on the home front in the spring of 1932. In Portland, Oregon, a group of unemployed veterans thought it might be a good idea to dramatize their plight by marching on to Washington in support of the Patman Bonus Bill. A year ago, Congress had passed a similar bill over

Hoover's veto which gave veterans up to fifty percent of their bonus.

"Hard times ate up that money," many veterans grumbled. "We want the other half."

"And we want it now," others chimed in.

"What I say is, let's go to Washington and let the government know how we feel!" And so this lonely band of hopeful veterans began their cross-country trek.

The idea caught on. Groups of sympathizers joined them on the way. Other caravans formed in other parts of the country, all heading for Washington. Most were bona fide veterans. Some were not. A few were trouble-makers. A handful were admitted Communists, eager to exploit what promised to be an explosive situation.

They drifted into the District of Columbia by the hundreds, then thousands. They lived in huts, shacks, and tents pitched on a dreary, swampy meadow called Anacostia Flats. Some even brought their wives and children along. "Might as well," they said, "there's nothin' for us to do back home, anyways. Here, leastways, we can get somethin' to eat." They called themselves the "Bonus Expeditionary Force," and even issued a daily newspaper, the *B.E.F. News*.

"We got no guns, no booze, no radicals, only gripes," their leaders insisted over and over again. "We want the President to hear them."

But the President steadfastly refused. In Hoover's view they were "supposed veterans, in considerable part organized and promoted by the Communists," and including "a large number of hoodlums and ex-convicts determined to raise a public nuisance." Under those circumstances, he'd have nothing to do with them.

But they did have one official friend in Washington, Police Commissioner Pelham D. Glassford, a former brigadier general who had served in France, along with thousands of these same Bonus Marchers. Glassford brought in food and supplies, donated recreation equipment and generally maintained a friendly relationship with the B.E.F.

Not so the administration. It continued to regard the presence of the veterans as a threat to the nation's capital. There was even a suggestion that machine guns be brought out when marchers crowded around the Capitol on June 17 as the Senate began voting on the bill. But Chief Glassford argued against a show of force, insisting his police could keep order. The veterans themselves were quiet and orderly. They stretched out patiently on the lawns surrounding Capitol Hill. Their mood remained hopeful, almost jovial.

Then word finally reached them by noon: the Senate had overwhelmingly voted down the bonus. For a moment an ugly silence settled over the crowd, followed by a growl of anger. Many of the veterans cursed aloud. Some beat their fists into their palms. A few turned their faces into the hot dry grass, the better to hide their despair.

B.E.F. leaders quickly took charge. After a few short speeches, the veterans sang a chorus of "America" as a show of loyalty to the government and shuffled quietly back to their makeshift barracks on the Anacostia Flats.

And still Hoover refused to receive their spokesmen.

However, Hoover was not without compassion. As he explained in his memoirs: "I asked Congressional committees to appropriate funds to buy tickets home for the legitimate veterans. This was done and some 6000 availed themselves of its aid, leaving about 5000 mixed hoodlums, ex-convicts, Communists and a minority of veterans in Washington." He did not add that the cost of these tickets was to be deducted from the bonus due them in 1945.

About half of the Bonus Marchers remained in Washington that summer, long after the Senate vote. After all, where else could they go? Things were bad all over. Thirteen million Americans were out of work, with more being laid off every day. The stock market, for those who cared, was scraping bottom. All over the country breadlines grew longer. When, on occasion, a few jobs were thrown open, the lines of men patiently waiting to apply for those jobs seemed to stretch to infinity.

"The greatest aid to efficiency of labor," industrialist Samuel Insull had once said, "is a long line of men waiting at the gate." Insull, in that summer of 1932, had been convicted of embezzling millions of dollars; he was now safely out on bail while the veterans were still milling around Washington, wondering what to do next.

This was the sort of emotional vacuum eagerly sought by the troublemakers. John T. Pace, an admitted Communist who later recanted, confessed his role in the scheme of things: "I led the left-wing or Communist section of the Bonus March. I was ordered by my Red superiors to provoke riots. I was told to use every trick to bring about bloodshed."

Bloodshed came, sickeningly, on July 28, the day Congress was set to adjourn. Failing to get a presidential audience, failing to get any kind of sympathy from administration spokesmen, the remnants of the B.E.F. clustered around Capitol Hill. That was when the District Police were ordered to clear out some abandoned buildings occupied by a group of veterans. They advanced on target just about noon, under a hot sun.

John Pace went into action at the same time. Under the pretense of self-protection, he ordered a hard core of his followers to rush the police. They responded by tearing up pavement bricks and hurling them at Glassford's men. A riot ensued. In the melee two policemen, beaten to the ground, fired to protect their lives and killed two marchers. Many policemen were injured. This was too much for the District's Board of Commissioners. They urgently appealed for help. The President quickly called on Federal troops to maintain law and order.

By late afternoon, before the fascinated gaze of bystanders who lined Pennsylvania Avenue, the United States Army advanced on the confused, bewildered Bonus Marchers. Four troops of cavalry, six tanks and a column of infantry, bayonets at the ready, made up the military force. At their head, mounted splendidly on a horse, rode the ramrod figure of Colonel Douglas MacArthur. One of his aides was Major Dwight Eisenhower. Another was George Patton, Jr.

"That mob," MacArthur later stated, "was a bad-looking mob. The gentleness, the consideration with which they had been treated had been mistaken for weakness, and they had come to the conclusion that they were about to take over in some arbitrary way either the direct control of the government or else to control it by indirect methods."

There was nothing weak or indirect about the action of his troops. First, they flushed out the downtown buildings of Bonus Marchers. Then they marched on Anacostia Flats. After giving its occupants an hour to vacate the area, the soldiers moved in, tossing tear gas bombs at sullen groups who refused to leave. The troops then set fire to the shacks, just to make sure none of the marchers would return in the dead of night. The hapless veterans, choking and gagging on tear gas, some with children in their arms, gave way. As a last defiant gesture, a few set fire to their own huts. Miraculously no one was killed, though hundreds were wounded.

The flames that cast a reddish glow over the Washington skyline that night were witnessed by millions of Americans thanks to newsreels and newspaper accounts. Sherwood Anderson and Waldo Frank, representing a group of outraged writers, called at the White House on August 10 to protest the use of military force against unarmed civilians.

"The President," a spokesman told them, "is extremely busy now. He regrets he has no time to see you. Perhaps another time, gentlemen, if you would care to make an appointment?"

The two visiting writers turned to go. As they crossed the White House lawn, they heard a group of children singing "Happy birthday to you . . . Happy birthday, President Hoover, happy birthday to you."

Herbert Hoover, that summer of the B.E.F. protest, had reached his fifty-eighth birthday.

THIRTEEN

CITIZEN INDIGNATION AGAINST THE ADMINISTRATION's handling of the Bonus Marchers poured into Capitol Hill all summer long. "Blunder" was the mildest term to assail the President's ears.

Actually, many Americans also resented the pressure tactics used by the veterans themselves. But they hardly went along with the use of tanks, troops and tear gas as answers to the marchers' demands. They preferred the ballot box.

The riots had taken place after both parties had selected candidates for the national elections that November. The Democrats had come up with a daring gamble: the astute governor of New York State, Franklin Delano Roosevelt, urbane, aristocratic, liberal and physically handicapped. A polio attack eleven years before had put him in braces and crutches. However, the disability had not affected his duties as governor. But as President? That was something else again.

There was no question as to the Grand Old Party's choice: the incumbent President. To nominate anyone else would have been an explicit admission that his policies had failed. The nomination was duly made and accepted by Hoover later that summer.

As the campaign got under way, the two faced each other like a couple of veteran prizefighters. Hoover, a portly, embattled, defiant champion, was grimly determined to defend his record against all comers. Roosevelt, on the other hand, gave the impression of a jovial, vigorous younger contender—he was only fifty at the time—whose genial manner could charm a voter right out of his political tree.

Both men were ably seconded by teams of experts. Hoover had the loyal backing of his Cabinet, all but Henry L. Stimson, who remained outside the arena. The President explained that Stimson, as Secretary of State, felt he must be neutral, then added with some annoyance, "He was the first Cabinet leader in history to take that view."

Roosevelt's strategy was supplied by his famous "Brain Trust." Led by Judge Samuel N. Rosenman, it included a host of university professors, among them Felix Frankfurter, Raymond Moley and Rexford Guy Tugwell.

It turned out to be a battle of words right from the beginning. Hoover launched the Republican attack with a strong position paper which he delivered in person on August 11 before a nationwide radio audience.

Roosevelt countered with a major speech nine days later.

Neither left voters in the dark as to the number one issue of the campaign, the Depression!

The Democratic strategy was simplicity itself: blame the Republicans for the boom, the bust and the Depression, then charge that Hoover did nothing to bail the country out. If a point had to be stretched, stretch it. Everything was fair in love, war and politics. The Democrats, out of the White House for a dozen years, wanted in and the time never seemed better than in the Fall of 1932.

The Republican grand design was equally blunt: deny, dispute and put the record straight. If a point had to be avoided, avoid it. After all, the administration never had a chance to prove what it could really do, what with one emergency after another. The voters owed it to themselves and the country to give the Republicans one more chance.

Hoover himself didn't seem to think they would get it. "By the nature of things," he recalled, "we were somewhat on the defensive as to certain issues." But taking heart, he quickly cheered himself with the thought that "we were able to take the offensive, especially on currency, tariff, the Supreme Court, and the collectivist planned economy."

There was nothing subtle about the give and take. Smiling, confident, strong-voiced, Franklin Roosevelt laid the issue squarely before the electorate, almost with a touch of insolence. "I sum up the history of the present administration in four sentences."

"First," Roosevelt said of the Hoover administration, "it encouraged speculation and overproduction, through its false economic policies.

"Second, it attempted to minimize the crash and misled the people as to its gravity.

"Third, it erroneously charged the cause to other nations of the world.

"And finally, it refused to recognize and correct the evils at home which had brought it forth; it delayed relief; it forgot reform."

Roosevelt himself conveniently left out a number of facts to the contrary: Hoover's warnings on speculation, his formation of the Reconstruction Finance Corporation, and his serious attempts to reform banking laws. But in a massive offensive, such details were easily overlooked.

The President, who often admitted that he hated to speak in public, could not match the challenger's verbal footwork. He delivered his speeches in his usual dry, detached manner, correct but dull, and frequently bowed down with verbiage. For example, defending his party's Depression policy, he said in part: "We have resolutely rejected the temptations, under pressure of immediate events, to resort to those panaceas and short cuts which, even if temporarily successful, would ultimately undermine and weaken what has been already molded by experience."

Noble ideas, big words, long sentences. Americans in factory towns, city slums and on farms had trouble following his rhetoric. Also, many of his listeners were out of work. They wanted action. Now take this Roosevelt; he kept talking about "the forgotten man at the bottom of the economic pyramid." That's us, by God, they agreed!

Why, he even called them "my friends"! And he sounded as if he meant it when he promised the nation a "New Deal."

Hoover took a somewhat waspish attitude toward the men who supplied the ammunition for Roosevelt's oratory. "Roosevelt," he observed, "delivered a multitude of speeches, some written by irresponsible or ignorant men." Not a very complimentary description of the "Brain Trust," which turned out most of the governor's public statements and included half a dozen professors of law, government and economics. However, as in many of Hoover's contentions, there was a core of truth in what he said.

One source which caused him no end of grief was Charles Michelson, a former reporter, and now national publicity director for the Democrats. For the past three years he had been sending out a barrage of anti-Hoover propaganda, not always in the best of taste and not always very close to the truth.

"Michelson," Hoover once remarked, "came out of the smear department of yellow journalism," thus wielding the brush a bit in his own right.

The publicist's job was to discredit the opposition in the news media, by no means a new technique in politics. The President must have known something about mud-slinging. He was, after all, well read in American history. Such notables as Thomas Nast, William Randolph Hearst, H. L. Mencken and Lincoln Steffens were all journalistic hatchet men in their time. The latter three, as a matter of fact, were very much alive during the campaign. Whether Michelson was in their class was something else again. As far as the Democrats were concerned, he was doing the job for which he was handsomely paid.

Hoover himself cloaked his own performance with a mantle of modesty. "During the campaign of 1932, I made only nine major speeches," he noted, and added virtuously, "moreover, I wrote my own speeches—and a proper presentation requires many days to prepare. I have never presented a ghost-written public statement of importance." Which was eminently true.

Furthermore, he knew he couldn't match Roosevelt in style, only in motives and logic. Hoover persistently argued against the charge that he had been a "do-nothing" President; he pointed to his farm policies, his relief committees, his public works program and his efforts in foreign affairs. But he had no comfortable answer for high tariffs, for the various committee reports which placed the problems of crime and the balanced budget ahead of unemployment, and for his party's support of Prohibition.

As the campaign progressed, the President explained with growing frustration, and some justification, that Roosevelt frequently spoke out of both sides of his mouth on a particular issue, that he told farmers one thing and factory workers another, that he catered to regional interests, that his programs, if adopted, would cost the nation billions of dollars. No matter; crowds cheered Roosevelt wildly wherever he appeared, whereas they were politely cordial to Hoover.

"I had little hope of re-election," the President admitted many years later.

But he kept up a brave front all that summer and fall. Then, as Election Day approached, Herbert and Lou Hoover headed for California. Like other citizens, the President and First Lady had an obligation to vote.

They spent the evening of November 7, 1932, at their Palo Alto home, surrounded by family and friends. As the polls closed in the East, the radio flashed the news to the West. The trend was obvious; the nation was going Democratic, but big! New York, Massachusetts, New Jersey in the East. Ohio, Illinois, Michigan in the Midwest. The South naturally—all were swept by the Democrats. Hoover salvaged only Pennsylvania and a few smaller states. The rout was complete when his home state, California, went to the other side. The final figures spoke volumes: 22.8 million votes for Roosevelt, 15.7 million for Hoover.

The defeated President studied the tally sheet once more then walked toward his study. "Time I sent the President-elect my congratulations."

As he returned, the night outside suddenly filled with the music of hundreds of youthful voices. A large group of Stanford University students had come to serenade the school's most distinguished alumnus. While torches flared, they sang all the college songs Herbert Hoover knew and loved so well.

The defeated champion reached for his wife's hand. "We owe them an appearance, Lou." He opened the large french doors leading to a balcony and waved at the students below. They responded by sending up a "locomotive" cheer, a long whistle followed by a rousing vocal explosion.

The President now stepped forward. The crowd suddenly fell silent. "I—I thank you all for your fine loyalty," he began, and for the first time the strain of the campaign showed in his voice. "I deeply appreciate this very hearty greeting." He struggled for more words, found none and ended up with a hoarse, "Thank you."

Then he moved back into the shadows. The President of the United States had retired for the night.

But not from public office. He still had to serve another four months before Franklin Delano Roosevelt, the papers were already referring to him as FDR, would take over the Presidency. Meantime the affairs of state had to be looked after.

On the way back to the nation's capital, the Hoovers stopped off at the Hoover Dam site near Las Vegas, Nevada. Ten years before, as Secretary of Commerce and chairman of the Colorado River Commission, Hoover had somehow pieced together an impossible jigsaw puzzle involving seven states and a dozen different pieces of legislation. The project was finally approved by Congress and named after the man who had done so much to get it started.

The dam was still a tangle of cement and pilings and scaffolding when the presidential party inspected it just after the 1932 elections. Hoover told an impromptu gathering of workmen, local officials and newspapermen that the dam represented the "greatest engineering work of its character ever attempted by the hand of man." Then he added, almost as an afterthought: "I should like to be present at its final completion as a bystander. Even so I shall feel a special personal satisfaction."

To the discredit of the succeeding administration, Herbert Hoover was never invited to the dedication ceremonies which marked the completion of the dam in 1936. Furthermore, it did not even bear his name at that time, having been changed by congressional action to Boulder Dam in mid-construction.

"I have never regarded the name as important," Hoover said, with obvious self-control. "The important thing is that it will bring happiness to millions."

Eventually, it brought him pride and satisfaction as well. In 1947, Congress restored its original name, Hoover Dam. It stands today as a monument to the engineering vision of the thirty-first President of the United States.

Chaos marked the lame duck session of Congress in the winter of 1933. With the Democrats in control, neither house took any action that would help the outgoing administration. Their motto, as one newspaper put it, might have been: "We will save the nation but sink Hoover."

This clumsy transitional period of four months, from Election Day to March 4, has since been cut in half. Thanks to the Twentieth Amendment, the President-elect is now sworn into office on January 20, a much more realistic interval. Ironically, Congress made the change in February 1933, but too late to help the Hoover administration.

At the time the waiting period was almost fatal. Roosevelt refused to go along with Hoover's pleas for cooperation. Meantime, the Depression worsened. More banks failed as rumors abounded that the incoming President would take the nation off the gold standard. Bank deposits were hurriedly withdrawn and placed under mattresses or in sugar bowls or sewn into the linings of clothes.

Hoover desperately tried to push through a bill that would keep more banks from going under. But the Democrats in Congress sat on their hands; or at least that's the way the Republicans viewed the action. More likely, as John Hicks pointed out, "Roosevelt consistently refused to commit his administration to anything in advance." As for those banking proposals, Professor Hicks explained "that the statements he [Hoover] had hoped to obtain from Roosevelt would have involved 'the abandonment of ninety percent of the so-called new deal.' "

Characteristically, Herbert Hoover arose early on March 4, 1933, breakfasted and went to his office as usual. He worked at his desk all morning until an aide reminded him it was time for the inauguration. Then Hoover got up, wrapped a muffler around his heavy shoulders, put on his overcoat and top hat and went out to greet Roosevelt. He knew it would be far easier for him to walk to his physically disabled successor than the other way around, as was the usual custom.

Thus Hoover left the Presidency not quite before his fifty-ninth birthday. And he left it under a cloud of the Democrats' making: that he and his administration were responsible for the Depression. An effective campaign issue had been twisted into fact. Hoover may not have done all he could to stop the Depression; some of his policies actually intensified it. But he did not *create* it. Even his most severe critics have agreed. They have admitted that Hoover remained the most high-minded of the New Era leaders in the age of business.

But if his critics had softened their judgments on him, as much could not be said of Hoover's own attitude toward the opposition. In a surprisingly harsh assessment following his defeat, Hoover stated: "My interest in my country could not be ended by an election, especially as I knew the character and purpose of the men coming into power were not those of traditional America."

FOURTEEN

An Inauguration Day photograph taken on the steps of the Capitol on March 4, 1933, reveals a glum-faced Hoover lost in thought while Chief Justice Hughes administers the oath of office to Franklin Delano Roosevelt. The deposed President might well have been reflecting on his own inauguration four years before and perhaps thinking: *If only I had been given another chance!*

He wrote something very much like the above in his autobiography. "I am so immodest as to believe that had we been continued in office we would have quickly overcome the Depression and approached economic and social problems from the point of view of correcting marginal abuse and not of inflicting a collectivist economy on the country."

In some quarters, this could be termed the reaction of a poor loser.

But defeat, even one of such proportions, wore off in time. Herbert and Lou Hoover spent the first few months of freedom doing absolutely nothing or everything; traveling about or staying put; sleeping late or staying up. In short, doing whatever pleased them without regard to protocol or pressure. Yet the ex-President could not remain idle for long. It was against his nature to loaf.

Furthermore, he had a mission in life: to expose the New Deal, which he labeled "a disaster to my countrymen." Accordingly, he and his wife divided the year between their home in Palo Alto and New York.

Hoover's initial target was the legislation passed during Roosevelt's first one hundred days in office. In the period of a little over three months, a compliant Congress gave the new President extraordinary powers to push through one emergency measure after another.

FDR began by ordering the nation's banks to close down for eight days. He felt he had to do this since so many had been failing, especially since mid-January. After Congress voted new and stronger banking regulations almost all re-opened in a matter of weeks.

Hoover's reaction was bitter. "It was the most political and most unnecessary bank panic in all history. It could have been prevented. It could have been cured by simple cooperation."

Some experts have cast doubts on this claim. More than 1300 banks had failed in 1930 and nearly 2300 in 1931, long before Roosevelt had a chance to cooperate as President-elect. There were another 1500 failures in 1932. But after 1933, bank failures diminished to almost nothing. Obviously, the Roosevelt administration must have been doing something right.

During those hundred days, Congress also passed the National Recovery Act (NRA), the Agricultural Adjustment Act (AAA), the Unemployment Relief Act, the Public Works Administration (later the WPA), the

Tennessee Valley Authority bill and a number of other important measures.

Hoover never let up in his attacks. He called these measures threats to private enterprise and individual freedom. But most Americans couldn't care less. They had seen almost four years of "private" measures, heard almost an unbroken string of optimistic remarks about how good times could be, if only! They were now far too absorbed in the daring performance of the New Deal.

The ex-President let out another alarm when Roosevelt devalued the dollar. Roosevelt did this by raising the price of gold from $21 an ounce to $35, thereby reducing the gold content of the American dollar to about sixty cents. This brought a large amount of foreign gold to the United States Treasury—about $15 billion in exchange for goods and assets. Hoover promptly dubbed this "currency tinkering" and called it a "sinister action."

He became equally incensed when Roosevelt recognized Soviet Russia in November 1933. Hoover charged that this action "was well designed to pull wool over American eyes."

The barrage against the New Deal continued. Hoover described FDR as leaning heavily to the "left" and claimed the left-wing group had become a dominant force in his administration. Roosevelt's program was an attempt to cross-breed Socialism, Fascism, and Free Enterprise, he said. Hoover also raised the specter of subversives in government, a tactic used later with devastating effect by Senator Joseph McCarthy, when he stated that "there were exposed, at one time or another, more than a thousand bad risks occupying important official positions in the Roosevelt administration."

As time went on, several of Roosevelt's close advisors quit his administration over real or fancied hurts and wrote their own impressions of the New Deal. The disenchanted included such former stalwarts as Jim Farley, Raymond Moley, Hugh Johnson, George Creel and John Nance Garner, who served for two terms as Vice-President under FDR. Hoover especially relished quoting from their versions of the truth.

"The books of all these men," he emphasized, "depict the Roosevelt policies and action bitterly."

The fact was indisputable that many government officials shuttled in and out of Washington during the 1930s. Some left because they clashed with Roosevelt's admittedly strong personality, some because of very real differences of opinion as to methods of operation, Hugh Johnson over the NRA, for example.

It's also worth noting that many more—by far the greater number—served the Roosevelt administration well and faithfully. In his assaults on the New Deal, Hoover seldom quoted from the journals of Harry Hopkins, Henry Wallace, Frances Perkins, Harold Ickes, Averell Harriman and others who were close to the White House.

Some of Hoover's fiercest blows fell on the hapless NRA. This emergency measure sought to boost economic recovery by putting a floor on wages and prices and a ceiling on hours. It also called for collective bargaining and union recognition by industry; for agriculture it advocated crop control. Hoover jumped on the bill as "monopolistic" and "sheer fascism."

On this particular target he had more company. First, Hugh Johnson. Then in 1935, the U. S. Supreme Court declared parts of the NRA unconstitutional since they delegated powers to the President that normally should rest with Congress.

"This is delegation running riot!" Supreme Court Justice Cardozo announced.

Herbert Hoover agreed heartily.

Yet such were the needs for NRA measures of the early 1930's that most of them were sooner or later incorporated into the American scene. Today, for example, minimum wages and maximum hours in industry are taken for granted. Collective bargaining is the rule, not the exception. Union recognition is an accomplished fact. Crop control is also very much part of the agricultural economy. company of dictators.

In spite of this, Hoover charged that the NRA "introduced to Americans the spectacle of Fascist dictation to business, labor and agriculture." *Fascist* was a word he used somewhat too easily.

Socialist was another. He directed this word particularly at the Tennessee Valley Authority, established by Congress in May 1933. "The effect of socialistic government competition," Hoover grimly said, "was to stifle finance in the private electrical utility field." For evidence, he cited annual figures: under the two previous Republican administrations, the electric power industry spent an average of $728 million a year for new construction, including the bad years; during 1933–1940, the annual average dropped to $303 million. But today, even with TVA, the Bonneville Power Authority, the Grand Coulee Dam and a half a dozen other governmentally operated power complexes, outlays by private electrical companies have averaged something like $40 billion a year. So much for "stifling" spending by private enterprise.

Hoover was very much in the political picture in 1936. Some even urged that he run again; in a rousing speech before the Republican Convention that year, he sounded as if he wanted to make a move in that direction. But nothing came of it as the Grand Old Party chose Alfred M. Landon, Governor of Kansas, as its standard bearer.

Hoover stumped for Landon without always agreeing with his policies, which, to him, smelled faintly of the New Deal. So he went his own way, reminding the nation that in spite of Federal spending, unemployment was still 11 million in 1936, or 10 or 9 million, depending on whose figures were used.

In trying to awaken voters, Hoover repeated the cry he had made at the convention. "Republicans and fellow Americans! This is your call . . . lead the attack to retake, recapture, and retain the citadels of liberty!" Oddly enough, his delivery had improved greatly since he left office.

In response to Hoover's plea, nearly 17 million Republicans and fellow Americans voted for Landon. But almost 28 million Democrats and other fellow Americans voted for Roosevelt. It was a stunning victory for the New Deal as every state in the union but two, Maine and Vermont, endorsed FDR for a second term.

It was also a shattering blow to Hoover's pride.

Parts of the New Deal, however, met with Hoover's approval, with certain reservations. He had a good word to say for Roosevelt's Home Owners Loan Corporation, which took pressure off mortgage payments, but he thought the government agency should deal through banks rather than directly with individuals. He also favored the Export-Import Bank created in 1934, but he added that it was later used for "political, economic and diplomatic pressures." And most surprising of all, Hoover gave his consent to the Social Security Act of 1935. This bill, then as now, provided for unemployment benefits, old-age pensions and aid to dependent children. "The broad objective of this act was meritorious," Hoover granted. Then came his "however." "The method of financing old-age pensions, however, was unsound." Thirty years later, after making payments of several billions dollars to some millions of elderly Americans, the Social Security Act has still to prove Hoover's contention that its financing was unsound.

While the New Deal struggled with recovery at home, a wave of political unrest swept through Europe. Adolf Hitler had come into power in Germany. Benito Mussolini had already carved out an empire in Africa. In Spain the legions of Franco successfully throttled the legally constituted government and set up a dictatorship in 1936.

Against this background of fascist take-over, Hoover used a most unfortunate association. "It has been the technique of all collectivist leaders," he wrote, "to single out some element of the community for concentrated hate. Lenin directed hate toward the 'bourgeoisie'; Hitler, toward the Jews; Mussolini, toward the Communists and democrats; Mr. Roosevelt concentrated . . . on a generalized class which he called 'economic royalists.' "

FDR never forgave Hoover for putting him into this company of dictators.

As war clouds rumbled over Europe in the late 1930s, Hoover warned America to remain aloof from military involvement. When Hitler marched into Poland on September 1, 1939, he urged caution. And when Germany invaded Russia in June 1940, he redoubled his efforts to keep America out of the war.

Those close to him held the opinion that he believed England could not be beaten, no matter what. "Especially," as Hoover publicly stated in October 1940, "if our . . . industry furnished them with all the guns and planes it is capable of producing."

And what about Russia, who was then fighting in the Ukraine and at the very gates of Moscow?

"If we go further and join the war and we win," Hoover reminded America on June 29, 1941, "then we have won for Stalin the grip of communism on Russia. Again I say, if we join the war and Stalin wins, we have aided him to impose more communism on Europe and the world. War alongside Stalin to impose freedom is more than a travesty. It is a tragedy."

He did not, at the time, suggest what tragedy might befall the world if Stalin lost and, presumably, Hitler won.

He was equally convinced that we should avoid war against Japan. Nor should we enter into any alliance with communism, he advised, in order to keep America strong and free for postwar leadership in making the peace.

Hoover held these views right up until the afternoon of December 7, 1941.

Immediately after the Japanese attack on Pearl Harbor, Herbert Hoover swept away all his foreign policy differences with Roosevelt. "We must fight with everything we have. I have opposed the foreign policies of our government. I believe alternate policies would have been better. Today there is just one job for the American people. We must defeat this invasion by Japan and we must fight it in any place that will defeat it. We must have and will have full support for the President of the United States."

But President Roosevelt, elected to an unprecedented third term the month before, gave no indication that he heard this plea for unity. At least he failed to call on Hoover for a role in the war effort, in spite of his proven leadership in previous emergencies.

Perhaps Roosevelt had a long memory and an unforgiving one. Perhaps he still remembered the man who had called him a "left-winger," who had linked his name to "wickedness" and "dictators," and who had repeatedly accused him of pushing through laws that smacked of "sheer fascism."

And so Herbert Hoover, still vigorous at sixty-seven, sat out World War II. He remained on the sidelines for four long years, much to his chagrin and, undoubtedly, to the nation's great loss.

For whatever might be said about Hoover's effectiveness in *elective* office, it was generally recognized that few men were his equal in an *appointive* post. All he had to be told about a job was "go ahead and do it." And it would be done.

FIFTEEN

ON FRIDAY, JANUARY 7, 1944, A COLD AND BITTER day in New York, Lou Henry Hoover hurried from a Girl Scout committee meeting to an afternoon concert in Carnegie Hall. Afterward she took a taxi to her apartment in the Waldorf-Astoria hotel.

Normally she would have walked the dozen blocks but she felt very tired that day, exhausted.

Her husband thought so, too, when she arrived home. He advised her to lie down, saying that he would look in on her as soon as he finished dressing since he had a function to attend later that evening.

Moments later, he knocked on her door. No answer. He knocked again, walked in and found her sprawled out on the floor, unconscious. Mrs. Hoover, nearly seventy years of age, had had a severe heart attack. In a few hours she was dead.

To the many thousands who later sent their condolences Hoover replied: "I had lived with the loyal and tender affection of an indomitable soul almost fifty years. Hers were those qualities which make a real lady."

But life, meanwhile, had to go on. Hoover lost himself in work, in his lectures and writing his memoirs. Like all other Americans, he followed the course of the war in Europe and the Pacific, a war which swung over to the Allied side after the invasion of Normandy on June 6, 1944. The Nazi surrender followed next spring. Months later, the war in the Pacific also came to a victorious close as Japan surrendered.

The aftermath of all major wars was hunger, chaos, disruption. No one knew that better than Hoover. So when President Harry S. Truman, who had succeeded Franklin Roosevelt upon the latter's death in April 1945, asked him to come to Washington for a conference on world famine, Hoover was delighted. On March 1, 1946, he returned to the White House after an exile of twenty-three years, almost to the day. It was homecoming in every sense of the word.

"Mr. President," he told Truman, "the last great reservoir from which starvation can be halted is in the United States. I am confident that the American people will respond to this great obligation, just as they did in the first World War."

After a series of conferences, Hoover led a group of experts on an inspection tour of world hunger spots. Two months, thirty-eight countries and thirty-five thousand miles later, they returned with their recommendations.

Hoover's report, Truman recalled, "outlined a country-by-country, month-by-month minimum program to the famine areas." This, he said, "was invaluable to me in planning the measures that had to be taken in the months ahead." As an immediate result, six million tons of American rice, wheat, and corn were shipped out to the hungry of the world. Within the year, the child-feeding program was taken over by the United Nations International Children's Emergency Fund, known today as UNICEF, to Hoover's entire satisfaction.

But a grateful Truman was not yet ready to send him back to the obscurity of private life. He therefore asked if he would undertake another study, this one dealing with the reorganization of government, which had grown to enormous proportions during and immediately after World War II.

The project had Hoover's complete sympathy. He himself had been anxious to streamline Federal functions as far back as 1929, only to have the Depression knock that program off the boards.

He agreed to head the commission as chairman provided he had a free hand to explore and recommend. He also asked that the committee be nonpartisan and small enough to be manageable. Both Truman and Congress respected his views. Accordingly, twelve men were named to the Hoover Commission in 1947, including Hoover himself. Its official title: The Commission on Organization of the Executive Branch of Government.

The road ahead was long, twisting and buried under tons of bureaucratic paperwork, a challenge made to order for Hoover's technically trained mind. As chairman, he appointed twenty-four task groups to study a similar number of government functions. Then they reported back to him for consultations, revisions and further action. The job completely absorbed his considerable talents over a period of two years.

In 1949, the Hoover Commission presented 273 proposals to Congress. The Truman administration acted on some of them at once; others were implemented by the Eisenhower administrations of 1952–1958.

The commission was called back for a second round in 1953 to handle a whole new set of problems growing out of the Korean conflict. Following another two years of study, Chairman Hoover put 314 more proposals before Congress. Government experts estimated that the first report saved taxpayers about $7 billion, while the savings from the second amounted to $3 billion.

The most important of the commission recommendations include the Military Unification Act of 1949, creation of the General Services Agency (a single purchasing unit in government), formation of the Department of Health, Education and Welfare, cost accounting and budget modernization, reduction of government competition in business, development of a Federal career service, coordination of Federal research, and reduction of red tape in general. Some proposals are still under study; all are aimed at making government less costly, better organized and more streamlined.

Or, as Hoover himself put it so well: "If the republic is not to be overwhelmed, the people must have such methods and systems as will enable good officials to give them good government."

Hoover's first report came just before his seventy-fifth birthday which was celebrated on August 10, 1949. It was an anniversary that breached two decades and a thousand memories, many pleasant, a few still rancorous, though less intense than during the Depression years.

The passage of time had muted many angry voices. The El Paso (Texas) *Times* wrote that Mr. Hoover "was wrong in 1930–31 . . . but . . . is just about right today. . . ." The *Press-Herald* in Portland, Maine, concurred: "He made mistakes during his White House tenure, as do all Presidents, but no one can question his high-mindedness and devotion to public service."

His birthday also drew praise from those who thought he had been right all along. "Few men, if any, in modern times," the Salt Lake City *Deseret News* of Utah, proclaimed, "have done more than he for the lasting benefit of his country and the world." The Omaha (Nebraska) *Herald* agreed, adding: "Herbert Hoover was a man of profound conviction, of warmest sympathy, a man above rancor and spite and partisanship, a man of granite integrity and surpassing ability. . . ."

Adulation was something new for this man. But aside from that quiet smile, and a soft spoken word of acknowledgment, Herbert Hoover found it difficult to respond. There was, after all, much work still to be done.

Writing occupied most of his later years. The ex-President completed his three-volume biography, *The Memoirs of Herbert Hoover,* in 1952. He added several more chapters to his *Addresses on the American Road,* the last of which was published in 1961. *The Ordeal of Woodrow Wilson,* which he finished in 1958, was hailed by critics as an impressive study of one great American by another.

Hoover had his lighter moments as well, even in print. His letters to and from children, *On Growing Up,* came out in 1962, and his delightful comments on his favorite sport, *Fishing for Fun and to Wash Your Soul,* were published the year after.

He was at work on a three-volume study on American-Soviet relations on his ninetieth birthday, which he, and the nation, celebrated on August 10, 1964. He stopped only long enough to nod at the familiar affectionate greetings, then went back to work.

He never finished his book. On October 20, 1964, at the age of ninety, Herbert Clark Hoover died peacefully, unable, for once, to answer the last, great challenge, to carry on.

He has left many shrines to honor his memory. Some forty schools throughout the country bear his name. There is a Herbert Hoover Library in West Branch, Iowa, which he dedicated on his eighty-eighth birthday. The Hoover Library for War, Revolution and Peace, started early in his political career and dedicated in 1941, is another monument to his memory, as is the great Hoover Dam, a giant among engineering projects of the world. The tiny cottage where he was born has been set aside as a national landmark.

He will be remembered for all these and more.

Yet his career was also witness to actions and attitudes less tangible but no less real. They include, most importantly, his lifelong struggle against Federal involvement in the life of the individual. Almost to the last, he defended personal freedom, as he saw it, against government encroachment in the conduct of business, labor, education, utilities, transportation, agriculture, old-age pensions, unemployment and medical care.

Herbert Hoover was convinced that these pursuits could best be carried on by enlightened private enterprise, under responsible self-regulation, and under local administration wherever possible. He saw Federal control of these activities as an invitation to dictatorship, corruption, waste and inefficiency. In his traditionalist view, they were violations of the Constitution.

Yet today many areas of American social and economic life are under some form of Federal supervision and operation, medicare, for example. Legislation concerning the food we grow and eat and sell, the pensions we collect in our old age, even payment for part of our burial costs, has been passed by the Congress of the United States. Bills of this nature have been signed into law by Presidents of both major political parties. And they have been upheld by the Judiciary and enforced by Federal agencies and officers.

The question remains—which will last longer as part of American civilization? The tangible monuments that honor the life and career of Herbert Clark Hoover? Or the struggles that he carried on in the name of liberty and freedom as interpreted by *his* view of the Constitution?

History—the companion of time—holds the answer.

INDEX

About the Author

JAMES P. TERZIAN was born on October 12, 1915, and grew up in New York City. A graduate of the University of Wisconsin, he worked his way through school as a radio news editor and sports announcer. Mr. Terzian was employed by the U.S. Information Agency's "Voice of America" for eight years following World War II, during which time he wrote a number of outstanding documentary programs for overseas broadcast. He has also written extensively for the United Nations, and is the author of magazine articles, film strips and movie scenarios.

A writer from his youth, Mr. Terzian's first published short story was cited in the "Best American Short Stories in 1934." He has since been named in that annual anthology in 1961 and 1964. He also won *Story Magazine's* "Best College Short Story" award in 1944. By then he was in the U.S. Navy Seabees as an enlisted combat correspondent. His account of the Japanese kamikaze on American naval ships appeared in the "Best War Stories of the Pacific."

Mr. Terzian is currently on the press relations staff of the Equitable Life Assurance Society. He lives in Chappaqua, New York, with his wife and youngest daughter.